THE LIBRARY
ST. MARY'S COLLEGE OF MARYLAND
ST. MARY'S CITY. MARYLAND 20686

W9-APB-215

CHILD DEVELOPMENT AND LEARNING THROUGH DANCE

AMS STUDIES IN EDUCATION: No. 7

ISSN 0882-438X

No. 1. Edmund W. Gordon and LaMar Miller, eds. *Equality of Equal Educational Opportunity: A Handbook of Research.* 1974.
No. 2. Francesco Cordasco, ed. *Toward Equal Educational Opportunity: The Report of the Select Committee on Equal Educational Opportunity, U. S. Senate.* 1974.
No. 3. Francesco Cordasco and William W. Brickman. *A Bibliography of American Educational History: An Annotated and Classified Guide.* 1975.
No. 4 Francesco Cordasco. *A Bibliography of Vocational Education: An Annotated Guide.* 1977.
No. 5. Charles Harrington. *Psychological Anthropology and Education: A Delineation of a Field of Inquiry.* 1979.
No. 6. V. Stevens, R. Sussex, and W. V. Tuman. *A Bibliography of Computer-Aided Language Learning.* 1986.

ABOUT THE AUTHOR

James H. Humphrey, Professor Emeritus at the University of Maryland is the author or co-author of 31 textbooks which have been adopted for use in over 1,200 colleges and universities. He has written 13 children's books and is the creator of 4 educational record albums. Two of his children's books on dance are widely used in the schools of the United States and Great Britain. Among his 200 articles and research reports are a number of writings on dance and rhythmic activities for children. Professor Humphrey is the founder and coeditor of *Dance: Current Selected Research* published annually, with the cooperation of the National Dance Association, by AMS Press, Inc.

CHILD DEVELOPMENT AND LEARNING THROUGH DANCE

James H. Humphrey

Foreword by
Lynnette Y. Overby

Coordinator of Dance Research
University of Maryland

AMS PRESS
New York

Library of Congress Cataloging-in-Publication Data

Humphrey, James Harry, 1911-
    Child development and learning through dance.

    (AMS studies in education; no. 7)
    Bibliography: p.
    Includes index.
    1. Dancing—Study and teaching (Elementary) 2. Child development. 3.
Movement education. 4. Perceptual-motor learning. I. Title. II. Series.
    GV1589.H86 1987   372.8   86-47832
    ISBN 0-404-12668-5

Copyright © 1987 by AMS Press, Inc.

Published by
AMS Press, Inc.
56 East 13th Street
New York, N.Y. 10003

MANUFACTURED IN THE UNITED STATES OF AMERICA

CONTENTS

FOREWORD

From the perspective of the dance teacher and researcher, I have found *Child Development and Learning through Dance* a valuable resource of theoretical and practical materials.

Dr. Humphrey's scholarly approach to the issue of dance in the elementary schools shows, on the basis of his own research, the current status of dance in the public school systems. While his data reveal a somewhat discouraging picture of dance education as fraught with inconsistencies in terminology, methodologies, and time allotment, he brightens the picture by presenting a holistic approach to child development and learning through the medium of dance activities.

Professors of teacher education courses in children's dance will find valuable and useful material in this book. Dr. Humphrey's system of classification into structured, semistructured, and unstructured dance forms, together with the more specific categorization of curricular, compensatory, and cognitive dance will provide the future dance teacher with the necessary foundations to evaluate the needs of a particular group and plan appropriate activities.

Practicing teachers of dance and physical education as well as classroom teachers will also find this text useful. The wealth of theoretical and practical materials can be used as a resource for future programs and a justification for those which already exist.

The implications of this text as just outlined make it a valuable addition to the field of children's dance.

Lynnette Y. Overby, Ph.D.
Coordinator of Dance Research
University of Maryland

PREFACE

It is well known that the field of dance is characterized by great diversity. This became luminously clear to me a good many years ago when I made a documentary analysis and found over 30 different classifications of children's dance. As in any field where such diversity exists, there is also a divergence of interest in certain activities. As an analogy, in the field of sport it is not uncommon to find a tennis enthusiast who has little or no interest in the game of volleyball, while the volleyball player may not aspire to engage in the game of tennis—this despite the fact that they are both "net games."

And so it is in the case of dance. In fact, I have known modern dancers to display some degree of disdain for such dance forms as folk and square dance. Similarly, it is not uncommon for some individuals in the area of children's dance to be interested only in creative dance, while others profess greatest interest in the more structured dance forms.

Since *Child Development and Learning through Dance* is designed primarily as a textbook for courses in dance for children, the content is wide in scope, covering a wide range of ideas, concepts, and dance forms. Thus insofar as possible, it displays some of the diversity mentioned above.

The initial chapter considers such concerns as terminology, status, and trends. Chapter 2 explores how total development of children can be obtained through dance. Chapter 3 involves teaching and learning, a feature of which is the application of principles of learning to the teaching of dance to children. In Chapter 4 my concepts of curricular dance, cognitive dance, and compensatory dance are discussed. Chapter 5 is concerned with dance curriculum and incorporates some principles of curriculum development, also furnishing criteria for the selection of curriculum content. Chapters 6, 7, and 8 are devoted to dance content, taking into account basic dance movements, creative dance, and structured dance forms. Chapters 9 and 10 explore the use of cognitive dance in helping children learn about reading and mathematics. The final chapter discusses how dance activities can be used to improve upon the ability of children to learn.

The selection of content was based upon the following criteria: (1) guidelines for children's dance provided by the National Dance Association, (2) my own personal surveys of state departments of education and selected school systems, (3) examination of several existing programs of professional preparation, and (4) introspection, in the form of my own personal experience in dealing with teachers and children in the area of dance.

A book is seldom the product of the author alone. Admittedly, the author does most of the things concerned with actually putting a book together. However, it is almost always true that many individuals participate, at least indirectly, in some way before a book is finally "put to bed." This volume is no exception.

To acknowledge everyone personally would be practically impossible—for example, the countless numbers of teachers and children with whom I have been involved over the years in the area of dance, to whom I would like to express a debt of gratitude collectively.

It is possible and practical, however, to cite certain sources personally.

I wish to extend my thanks to Kimbo Educational of Long Branch, New Jersey for granting permission for me to use some of my own materials from *Teaching Reading Through Creative Movement,* and *Teaching Children Mathematics Through Games, Rhythms and Stunts.*

The following individuals shared knowledge with me on which certain parts of the book were based which would otherwise have been impossible: Virginia Moore, former Supervisor of Elementary Education, Anne Arundel County, Maryland Public Schools, Robert

Ashlock, former Director of the Arithmetic Center at the University of Maryland, Robert Wilson, Director of the Reading Center at the University of Maryland, and Dorothy Sullivan, former Associate Professor of Education at the University of Maryland. At one time or another all these individuals have been co-authors with me on a variety of writing projects.

Finally, I have had the benefit of important input from several notables in the area of children's dance. They are: Gladys Andrews Fleming, Judith Lynne Hanna, Theresa Purcell, Susan W. Stinson, and Lynnette Y. Overby. I am particularly grateful to the latter, who read the material from the point of view of the dance teacher/researcher and prepared the Foreword.

CHAPTER 1

BASIC CONSIDERATIONS OF DANCE FOR CHILDREN

It is the purpose of this book to examine the potential contribution of dance to the developmental processes and learning of children in the age and grade ranges which are comprised by the elementary school. The ages range from approximately five to approximately twelve, and the grade levels from kindergarten through grade six. The following scale show the approximate ages of children at the various grade levels.

Grade	Age
Kindergarten	5 to 6 years
First Grade	6 to 7 years
Second Grade	7 to 8 years
Third Grade	8 to 9 years
Fourth Grade	9 to 10 years
Fifth Grade	10 to 11 years
Sixth Grade	11 to 12 years

This initial chapter will take the following basic aspects of children's dance into account: (1) criteria for content of the book, (2) meaning

1

of terms, (3) dance and movement, and (4) classification of dance activities, (5) accompaniment for dance, and (6) status and trends in dance for children.

CRITERIA FOR CONTENT OF THE BOOK

It seems important at the outset to explain the criteria used as a basis for what the book contains, in order to establish an immediate author–reader rapport. The reader will then be in a more favorable position to judge the book by using these criteria for a valid appraisal and evaluation of it. The following criteria were used:

1. *Recommendations of the National Dance Association Task Force on Dance for Children.* This task force was spearheaded by one of my professional friends of long standing, Dr. Gladys Andrews Fleming. As its chairwoman she was instrumental in bringing to fruition the publication *Children's Dance,*[1] which contains many important recommendations for the dance education of children. A leader in the forefront of the field of dance, Dr. Fleming authored one of the most outstanding books ever published in this area. Her *Creative Rhythmic Movement* first published by Prentice-Hall in 1954 and revised over two decades later, has stood as a classical monument for teachers and others interested in providing dance experience for children.

The Task Force has provided important guidelines for those who wish to inaugurate new programs or implement and improve current programs of dance for children. As far as curriculum content is concerned the Task Force recommended such experiences as basic rhythms, creative dance, movement songs, and ethnic and folk dance, all of which are included in the content of this book. Emphasis was also placed on the importance of methods of teaching dance to children, giving major consideration to the so-called discovery and problem-solving methods. This of course means that the teaching of dance to children should be based on what is known about how children learn. With this in mind I have prepared a chapter which includes

---

[1] American Alliance for Health, Physical Education, Recreation and Dance, *Children's Dance,* revised edition, Washington, D.C., 1981.

the application of principles of learning to the teaching of children's dance.

In summary, the guidelines of this Task Force have been of considerable value as an important criterion in the preparation of this book.

2. *Surveys of state departments of education and selected school systems.* The extensive surveys that I have conducted over the last several years have yielded some valuable information as far as the content of the book is concerned. The purpose of the survey of state departments of education was to determine those classifications of dance activities most often used in the school systems of the various states. In this survey, for which 84% of the state representatives responded, the most frequently used at the primary level were fundamental rhythms, singing games (movement songs), creative dance, and folk and square dances. At the upper elementary level, as expected, folk dances, square dances, and creative dance were reported to be the most popular forms. Less frequent at both levels were modern dance clog and tap dancing, and ballet. Also reported were the use of such rhythmic activities as ball handling and rope jumping to accompaniment.

The surveys of approximately 100 selected school systems were conducted to find out the amount of time ordinarily spent in the various categories of dance activities, responsibility for teaching, and specific dances that were used most frequently. These data will be reported in appropriate places throughout the book.

3. *Examination of programs.* Over 80 physical education programs that provide specialized preparation for the elementary-school level were examined to determine the type of content offered in courses in the area of dance for children. All of these programs offered one or at the most two courses ranging from 2 to 4 credit hours.

The titles of these courses varied to the extent that over 50 different course titles were identified. In slightly over 42% of the cases the term *dance* only was used in the title and in about 35% of the cases the term *rhythm* only was used. In 15% of the cases both terms, dance and rhythm, were used, e.g. "Rhythms and Dance for the Elementary School Child." Specific forms of dance used in the titles were "creative" (9% of the time), "folk" (4%), and "American," "square," "modern," and "educational" (slightly more than 1%). The most popular course title, "Dance for Children," was used in 10% of the courses.

There was a wide range of course content, from "simple rhythms" to "complex structured dances."

4. *Introspection.* Some of my own most rewarding personal experiences with children have been in the teaching of dance activities. Whether it was the observation of a child's excitement in creating a movement inspired by a particular form of accompaniment, or of the joy they experienced in twisting and turning in a given dance pattern, I was always able to gain a better understanding of children as they engaged in these enjoyable activities.

MEANING OF TERMS

To avoid confusion it seems appropriate to convey to the reader the meaning of certain terms. A starting point for discussion might be the use of such terms in the title of this book as *development, learning,* and *dance.*

Development is concerned with changes in the child's ability to function at an increasingly higher level. For example, a stage in the development of the infant is from creeping to crawling. This is later followed by the developmental stage of walking when the child moves to an upright position and begins to propel himself over the surface area by putting one foot in front of the other. (This example is concerned with physical development but, as we shall see in the next chapter, there are other important forms of development, such as social, emotional, and intellectual).

Most definitions of *learning* are characterized by the idea that it involves some sort of change in the individual. This means that when an individual has learned, his behavior is modified in one or more ways. Thus, a good standard for learning would be that after having an experience a person should be able to behave in a way in which he could not have behaved before having had the experience. In this general connection, many learning theorists point out that while it is not possible to *see* learning, behavior can be seen, and therefore that when a change in behavior has occurred, it is possible to infer that change and learning have occurred. The essential different between development and learning is that development deals with general abilities, while learning is concerned with specific behaviors.

There has been some confusion with the terms *dance* and *rhythm*. A more or less common definition of *to dance is: to perform a rhythmic and patterned succession of bodily movements, usually to musical accompaniment*. If one accepts this definition then it is seen that rhythm is an essential factor in dance. Not only that, but one need only look to the functions of the human body to see the importance of rhythm in the life of young children. The heart beats in rhythm, the digestive processes function in rhythm, breathing occurs in rhythm; in fact, almost anything in which human beings are involved is done in a rhythmic pattern.

A question that sometimes arises is: Which is broader in scope—dance or rhythm? For my own part, I would place all human movement experiences that *require* some sort of rhythmical accompaniment under the broad category of rhythmic activities. On the other hand, although accompaniment is important in most dance activities, there are some forms of creative dance where it is not necessary. It becomes more or less an arbitrary matter because there are certain human movement experiences that require some sort of rhythmical accompaniment although they do not necessarily have the same objectives as those associated with dance.

In recent years a great deal of emphasis has been placed on what is called *aerobic* dancing. The term aerobic derives from the Greek word *aēr* which means "air." The purpose of aerobic dancing is said to be to strengthen the lungs, heart, and cardiovascular system as a whole. There are many spirited types of dances, such as square dance, that can accomplish this; indeed it could be said in general that any dance activity that causes one to "puff" hard enough could fall into the category of aerobic dancing. Therefore, it does not seem appropriate to label any particular form of dancing "aerobic" as distinct from other types of dances.

In recent years the area called aerobic dance has come under severe criticism. In fact, some dance educators have argued that in the large classes taught at the university level the worst of alignment and movement habits are practiced, resulting in a large number of injuries to participants. Apparently this has been such a problem that some are recommending what they refer to as "soft" aerobics.

It is interesting to note that at least one study[2] has shown, that participation in a university aerobic dance program did not improve students' cardiovascular fitness, and further, that aerobic instructors should be trained in the use of pulse rate and other principles of exercise physiology in order to make their work more effective.

Another form of dance that has gained favor with several enthusiasts is called *educational* dance. It was probably developed by Rudolph Laban, who is usually considered to be the "Father" of modern dance.[3] The modifying term *educational* is perhaps unfortunate. My my own opinion is that *all* dance for children is, or should be, educational. To isolate a specific form and call it educational could conceivably convey the impression that creative dance, movement songs, folk dance, and the like are less than acceptable in providing suitable educational experiences for children.

So much for terminology of a more or less general nature. Other terms will be described and elaborated where necessary.

DANCE AND MOVEMENT

Another basic consideration is one that takes into account *movement as a basis for dance.* Just as the perception of symbols is associated with reading readiness, so is basic movement an important factor in readiness to perform various kinds of dance activities. Since proficient performance of dance activities depends upon skill of body movement, the ability of the child to move effectively should be readily discerned.

[2] Pamela J. Russell, "Aerobic Dance Exercise Programs: Maintaining Quality and Effectiveness," *Physical Educator,* October 1983.
[3] Laban, Rudolph, *Modern Educational Dance,* 3rd ed., London, MacDonald & Evans, 1975.

Sometimes at a very early age a child may discover and use combinations of movements that in reality are (or will eventuate into) specialized motor skills normally used in the complex organization of a dance. In this sense, the child is becoming ready for direct skill teaching and learning. With proper teacher guidance, the basic movements that children develop on their own can be improved in accordance with proper principles of body mechanics and commensurate with their natural ability. The important factor is that in the early stages the child is made to feel comfortable with the way he or she moves and is thus in a better position to learn correct performance of skills. (Chapter 6 is devoted to basic dance movements).

CLASSIFICATION OF DANCE ACTIVITIES

Several years ago I conducted an extensive examination of the literature on children's dance in order to determine the various ways in which dance activities might be classified. This information yielded the following classifications:

1. Activity songs and poems
2. American dances
3. American Indian dances
4. Choral reading
5. Clog dancing
6. Couple dances
7. Creative dances
8. Creative rhythms
9. Customs dances
10. Dramatization
11. Folk dances
12. Free-response rhythms
13. Fundamental rhythms
14. Greeting and meeting dances
15. Gymnastic dancing
16. Imitative rhythms
17. International dances
18. Interpretative rhythms
19. Mimetic rhythms
20. Mixers
21. Modern dance
22. Nursery rhymes
23. Play-party games
24. Rhythm bands
25. Round dances
26. Singing games
27. Skill dances
28. Social dances
29. Square dances
30. Story rhythms
31. Tap dancing
32. Trade dances

Classification of dance activities into certain broad categories is difficult, owing in part to inconsistencies in the use of terminology to describe certain activities. For example, the above list shows no unifying principle of classification, but indiscriminately includes categories based on national and ethnic origin, formal genre, structural organization, educational purpose, etc. Thus, any attempt at classification tends to become somewhat arbitrary and is likely to be based on the experience, personal feelings, and purpose of the particular person doing the classifying.

When attempts are made to classify activities within a broad category it should be kept in mind that a certain amount of overlapping is unavoidable and that in some instances activities may fit well into more than one category. Another important consideration is that in some cases different names may be given to the same activity—an example of the inconsistencies in terminology mentioned previously. For example, in the above list, "creative rhythms" and "free-response rhythms" might be considered one and the same thing.

The approach to classification of dance activities that I like to use centers around the kings of dance experiences that one might wish children to have. It is suggested here that these experiences consist of (1) unstructured experiences, (2) semistructured experiences, and (3) structured experiences. It should be understood that in this particular way of grouping dance experiences, a certain amount of overlapping will occur as far as the degree of structuring is concerned; that is, although an experience is classified as unstructured, there might be a small degree of structuring in certain kinds of situations. With this idea in mind the following descriptions of these three types of dance experiences are submitted:

Unstructured experiences include those where there is an original or creative response in which there has been little, if any, previous explanation or discussion in the form of specified directions. The *semistructured* experiences comprise definite movements or interpretations suggested by the teacher, child, or a group of children. *Structured* experiences involve the more difficult dance patterns associated with various types of dances. A *well-balanced* program of dance activities for children would provide opportunities for these various types of dance experiences. Subsequent chapters will take these kinds of experiences into account.

FORMS OF ACCOMPANIMENT

There are many different forms of accompaniment suitable for use with dance activities. All of these can be useful when employed under the right conditions. At the same time all of them have certain disadvantages. In the final analysis it will be up to the teacher to select the form of accompaniment that will best meet the needs of a particular situation.

Five forms of accompaniment for dance activities are presented here along with what might be considered the advantages and disadvantages of each.

1. *Clapping* as a form of accompaniment can be useful in helping children gain a better understanding of tempo. There is also something to be said for the child actually becoming a part of the accompaniment on a physical basis, since it gives him a feeling that he is more involved. This is particularly important in the early stages when dance activities are being introduced. Clapping can be done with the hands or by slapping various parts of the body such as the knees and thighs. A major disadvantage of clapping as a form of accompaniment is that it is virtually impossible to obtain a melody through this procedure.

2. Various kinds of percussion instruments may be used as accompaniment, the most prominent being the *drum*. The drum is an instrument that is easy to learn and the person furnishing the accompaniment can change the tempo as he or she wishes. Some kinds of dances, such as some of the Indian dances, actually require the use of a drum as accompaniment. As if the case with clapping, the use of the drum makes it difficult to have a melody with the accompaniment.

3. *Singing* as a form of accompaniment is ordinarily required in movement songs and in square dances where singing calls are used. All children can become involved, as in the case of clapping. One of

the disadvantages of singing as a form of accompaniment is that the singing voices may become weaker as the children participate in the activity. For example, if movement songs require a great deal of skipping, it is difficult for the child to do both tasks, singing and skipping, for a very long period of time.

4. At one time the *piano* was a very popular form of accompaniment for dance activities. The chief disadvantage of the piano is that it is not the easiest of instruments to play, and not all the teachers have included it as a part of their professional preparation. Another disadvantage is that even if one is an accomplished pianist, the player must obviously be at the piano and thus away from the activity. The piano has the advantage that a melody can be obtained from it.

5. Perhaps the most popular form of accompaniment at the present time is *recordings*. Sources of this form of accompaniment are so plentiful that almost any kind of accompaniment can be provided. One disadvantage of recordings pertains to those that furnish instructions intended for children. Sometimes these instructions are confusing and too difficult for younger children to understand. The teacher should evaluate such instruction and determine whether this is the case. If it is found that the instructions are not acceptable for a particular group of children, the teacher can use the musical accompaniment on its own. The major advantage of recordings is that they are professionally prepared. However, teachers might well consider using a tape recorder to record their own music or singing voices of children as a form of accompaniment. (The Appendix provides a list of representative sources of recorded accompaniment for dance activities.)

STATUS AND TRENDS IN DANCE FOR CHILDREN

Dance for children has travelled an interesting and sometimes strange road. It is difficult to identify a precise time when dance activities were introduced into the elementary schools of America. Perhaps one of the earlier attempts in this direction came around the turn of the century when John Dewey was Director of the University of Chicago Laboratory Schools. At this time Dewey had introduced folk dancing into the program, and this may be the first time such an activity took place on such a formalized basis. Up until then, dance activities, if used at all, undoubtedly took place at sporadic intervals. For example, there were instances when certain types of singing games were a part of the "opening exercises" of some elementary schools.

During the decade preceding World War I some aspects of nationality dances found their way into the school program. This ordinarily occurred in those large cities where certain ethnic backgrounds were predominant in a given neighborhood.

The period between the two world wars saw dance activities introduced into more schools, and this was probably due to the fact that more emphasis was beginning to be placed on the social aspect of education. By the late 1920s some elementary schools were allotting as much as 25% of the total physical education time to dance activities, particularly at the primary level. This situation tended to prevail for some time after World War II.

It is interesting to note that certain adult dances "of the times" tend to have an influence on children of almost all ages. A case in point was the introduction of the *axials* in the form of the "twist" as a kind of dancing in the early 1960s by the young adult population. Many children of upper elementary school age likewise became interested in this approach to dancing. As a result some children began to rebel against some of the more traditional forms of dancing. On a lesser scale this same situation is prevailing in some instances with the previously mentioned "aerobic dancing."

In modern times dance activities in elementary schools are characterized by great diversity. There appears to be a wide variety of activities but little standardization from one school to another. The two major reasons for this are the variation in teacher preparation and the reluctance on the part of some teachers to teach these kinds of activities.

Although many dance enthusiasts would like to see dance established as a more or less separate entity in elementary schools, this attitude has met with relatively limited acceptance.

Recently, I conduced a survey of communities with a population of 500,000 or more, in an attempt to determine the assignment of responsibility for teaching dance in elementary schools. Sixty percent responded to the inquiry and the results are shown in the following table.

	Major Responsibility	Some Responsibility	No Responsibility
physical education teacher	34%	33%	33%
classroom teacher	33%	42%	25%
music teacher	11%	56%	33%
special dance teacher	0%	12%	88%

In another survey of over 900 elementary schools with more than one half million children and some 17,000 teachers, only one dance teacher was identified. This person wass supported by a fine arts grant and was not a regular member of the teaching staff.

One of the factors that tends to militate against the use of special dance teachers in elementary schools is the problem associated with state certification. At this writing I have been able to identify only ten states that have certification of dance teachers, and most of these are for the secondary school only.

Dance activities, when they are provided, tend to be considered a part of the broad area of physical education. My extensive surveys have shown that at the primary level about 20% of the physical education time is allotted to dance activities, and about 15% of the time at the upper elementary level.

While more or less traditional dance activities tend to be used, there appears to be a slight trend in the direction of more extensive use of creative dance at all of the elementary school grade levels. Nevertheless, I have found in my interviews that elementary-school physical education teachers, when asked what they are doing with creative dance, typically answer, "Not as much as I should."

Lest the reader discern gloom and doom as far as the status and trends in children's dance is concerned, let me hasten to mention that anything as important in the lives of children as dance will eventually prevail in some manner. Many dedicated individuals have been working and continue to work toward this goal.

CHAPTER 2

TOTAL CHILD DEVELOPMENT THROUGH DANCE

In order to make a valid exploration of the area of dance in the elementary school curriculum, it becomes necessary to consider the guiding philosophy and purpose of the elementary school as a whole, since it is clear that the guiding philosophy of the entire educational program should also apply to dance for children.

If one were to analyze the various statements of the purpose of elementary education which have been made by responsible educational agencies and groups, it would be relatively easy to identify a constantly emerging pattern. These statements through the years have gradually evolved into a more or less general agreement among present-day childhood educational leaders that the goal of elementary education is to stimulate and guide the development of an individual so that he or she will function in life activities involving vocation, citizenship, and enriched leisure; and, further, so that he or she will possess as high a level of physical, social, emotional, and intellectual well-being as his or her individual capacity will permit. More succinctly stated, the purpose of elementary education in our modern society should be in the direction of *total development* of the child during the formative years, which include kindergarten through grade six.

The ensuing sections of this chapter should be read with this general frame of reference in mind. This is to say that if it is a valid assumption that the purpose of elementary education is to attempt to insure total development of children, then it is incumbent upon us to explore the developmental processes as they relate to dance.

When it is considered that development of children brings about needs, and that these needs must be met satisfactorily, the importance of an understanding of development is readily discerned. When an understanding of the various aspects of development is achieved, one is then in a better position to provide improved procedures for meeting the needs of each individual child. This implies that we ought to be guided by what could be called a *developmental philosophy* if we expect to meet with any degree of success in our dealings with children.

FORMS OF DEVELOPMENT

As mentioned, total development is the fundamental purpose of the education of children. All attempts at such education should take into account a combination of *physical, social, emotional* and *intellectual* aspects of human behavior. In fact, the *Dictionary of Education* defines the term *child development* as *an interdisciplinary approach to the study of children, drawing upon such sciences as biology, physiology, embryology, pediatrics, sociology, psychiatry, anthropology, and psychology; emphasis is placed on the importance of understanding children through the study of their mental, emotional, social and physical growth; particular emphasis is laid on the appraisal of the impacts on the growing personality of home, school, and community.*[1]

Thus I will consider forms of development according to their physical, social, emotional, and intellectual aspects. Of course, there are other forms of development, but perhaps they can be subclassified under one of the above headings. For example, *motor development*, which can be defined as a progressive change in motor performance,

[1] Carter, Good, *Dictionary of Education*, 2nd ed., (New York: McGraw-Hill, 1959), p. 167.

is part of the broader category *physical development*. In addition, *moral development*, which is concerned with the capacity of the individual to distinguish between standards of right and wrong, could be considered one dimension of the broader area *social development*. This is to say that moral development, involving achievement in ability to determine right from wrong, is influential in the individual's social behavior.

It seems appropriate at this point to comment on other terminology that is often used by dance educators to describe forms of development. Reference is made to what are ordinarily considered the *learning domains*. These consist of the *affective* domain, the *cognitive* domain, and the *psychomotor* domain. Some writers refer to these as forms of development, i.e., affective development, cognitive development, and psychomotor development. In this frame of reference, affective development is ordinarily thought of as being concerned with "appreciation" of dance movement and is sometimes referred to as a combination of social and emotional development. Cognitive development in this context means knowledge about dance movement, or understanding why the body moves the way it does in certain dance activities. Psychomotor development involves learning to move with control and efficiency, or more simply stated, skill in dance movement.

TOTAL PERSONALITY

A great deal of clinical and experimental evidence indicates that a human being must be considered as a whole and not a collection of parts. For present purposes I would prefer to use the term *total personality* in referring to the child as a unified individual or total being. Perhaps a more common term is *whole child*. The term total personality, however, is commonly used in the fields of mental health and psychology and recently has been gaining more use in education. Moreover, when it is considered from a point of man existing as a person it is interesting to note that "existence as a person" is one rather common definition of personality.

The total personality consists of the sum of the physical, social, emotional, and intellectual aspects of any individual, i.e., the major forms of development previously identified. The total personality is "one thing" comprising these various major aspects. All of these components are highly interrelated and interdependent. All are of importance to the balance and health of the personality, because only in terms of their health can the personality as a whole maintain a completely healthful state. The condition of any one aspect affects another aspect to a degree and thus the personality as a whole.

When a nervous child stutters or becomes nauseated, this is not necessarily a mental state causing a physical symptom. On the contrary, a pressure imposed upon the organism causes a series of reactions, which include thought, verbalization, digestive processes, and muscular function. It is not that the mind causes the body to become upset; the total organism is upset by a situation and reflects its upset in several ways, including disturbance in thought, feeling, and bodily processes. The whole individual responds in interaction with the social and physical environment; and, as the individual is affected by the environment, he or she in turn has an effect upon it.

However, because of long tradition during which either physical development *or* intellectual development has been glorified, rather than both physical *and* intellectual development, we still often find ourselves dividing the two in our thinking. The result of this kind of thinking may be that we sometimes pull human beings apart.

Traditional attitudes that separate the mind and body tend to lead to unbalanced development of the child with respect to mind and body and/or social adjustment. What is more unfortunate is that we fail to utilize the strengths of one to serve the needs of the other.

In the foregoing statements I have attempted rather forcefully to present the idea that the identified components of the total personality comprise the unified individual. The fact that each of these aspects might well be considered as a separate entity should also be taken into account: each aspect, as such, would then warrant a separate discussion. This is extremely important if one is to understand fully the place of each as an integral part of the whole personality. The following discussions of the physical, social, emotional, and intellectual aspects of personality as they relate to dance for children should be viewed within this general frame of reference.

PHYSICAL DEVELOPMENT

One point of departure in discussing physical development might be to state that "everybody has a body." Some are short, some are tall, some are lean, and some are fat. Children come in different sizes, but all of them are born with a certain capacity that is influenced by the environment.

It might be said of the child that he "is" his body. It is something he can see. It is his base of operation. The other components of the total personality—social, emotional and intellectual—are somewhat vague as far as the child is concerned. Although these are manifested in various ways, children do not always see them as concretely as they do the physical. Consequently, it is important that a child be helped early in life to gain control over the physical aspects of personality, or what is known as *basic body control*—something that can be readily accomplished through dance. The ability to do this, of course, will vary from one child to another. It will likely depend upon the physical fitness of the child. The broad area of physical fitness can be broken down into certain components, and it is important that individuals make use of these components to achieve as much as their natural ability permits. While there is no complete agreement as to the identity of the components of physical fitness, the President's Council on Physical Fitness and Sports considers them to consist of muscular strength, endurance, and power; circulatory-respiratory endurance; agility; speed; flexibility; balance and coordination.[2]

The components of physical fitness, and thus of physical development, can be measured by calibrated instruments, as in measurements of muscular strength. Moreover, we can tell how tall a child is or how heavy or or she is at any stage of his or her development. In addition, other accurate data can be derived through assessments of blood pressure, blood counts, urinalysis, and the like.

[2] *Physical Fitness Research Digest,* President's Council on Physical Fitness and Sports, Washington, D.C., series No. 1, July 1971.

Guidelines for Physical Development Through Dance

It is imperative to set forth some guidelines for physical development if we are to provide for the proper physical development of children through dance. The reason for this is to assure, at least to some extent, that our efforts in attaining optimum physical development through dance will be based upon a scientific approach. These guidelines might well take the form of valid *concepts of physical development*. This approach enables us to give serious consideration to what is known about how children grow and develop. Thus, we can select dance experiences that are compatible with the physical developmental process. The following is a list of concepts of physical development, together with some of their implications for dance.

1. *Physical development and change is continuous, orderly, progressive, and differentiated.* In the early years, dance experiences ought to be characterized by large muscle activities. As the child develops, more difficult types of dance skills can be introduced, so that dance experiences progress in a way that is compatible with the child's development.
2. *Physical development is controlled by both heredity and environment.* The dance program should be planned in such a way as to develop the innate potential of each child. Attempts should be made to establish an environment in which all children have an equal opportunity for wholesome participation.
3. *Differences in physical development occur at each age level.* This implies that there should be a wide variety of activities to meet the needs of children at various developmental levels. In gearing dance activities to meet the needs of a particular group of children, attempts should also be made to provide for individual differences within the group.
4. *Needs of a physical nature must be satisfied if a child is to function effectively.* Dance experiences should be planned to provide an adequate activity yield. Dance programs should be vigorous enough to meet the physical needs of children and at the same time sufficiently motivating to make them desire to perpetuate the dance experience outside of school.

5. *Various parts of the body develop at different rates and different ages.* Undue strain to the point of excessive fatigue should be avoided in dance activities. Teachers should be aware of fatigue symptoms in order that children not be pushed beyond their physical capacity. Perhaps the use of large muscles should predominate in dance activities, at least for primary-level children.

6. *The individual's own growth pattern will vary from that of others, both as to time and rate.* It might be well to compare a child's performance with his or her own previous achievements rather than that of classmates. It should be recognized that the same standards of performance cannot be expected from all children in any given activity, due to individual differences.

7. *There are early maturers and late maturers.* This concept suggests the importance of the proper grouping of children within given dance classes. The teacher should know when it will be more profitable to classify children homogeneously and when heterogeneously for certain kinds of dance experiences.

8. *The level of physical maturation of the child often has a significant effect on learning.* Very young children should not be expected to achieve beyond their ability levels.

9. *Physical differences may have a marked effect on personality.* A variety of dance experiences should be provided, in an effort to give each child a chance to find some successful physical achievement within his or her own physical capacity. The teacher should set the example for children to learn to be respectful of physical differences by helping them make use of their particular body type in the most advantageous way.

When dance programs for children are planned and implemented on the basis of what is known about how they grow and develop, there is a greater likelihood that worthwhile contributions can be made to physical development. Adherence to valid concepts of physical development is considered one of the best ways of accomplishing this goal.

What Should Dance Do for Children Physically?

There is an abundance of scientific evidence to indicate that well-planned physical activity such as dance is a stimulant to physical growth. Moreover, it has been my own personal experience that participation in a well-balanced dance program is one of the best ways of maintaining optimum health. In reality, then, a well-balanced dance program should help children gain strength, endurance, agility, coordination, and flexibility commensurate with the energy required for a successful and happy present and future life. A program of this nature implies that every child be given the opportunity to develop skills and abilities to the best of his or her individual physical capacity. This is essential if each individual is to derive full benefit and optimum enjoyment from participation in dance activities.

SOCIAL DEVELOPMENT

Human beings are social beings. They work together for the benefit of society. They have fought together in time of national emergencies in order to preserve the kind of society they believe in and, yes, many of them have enjoyed the experience of dancing together. Despite all this, the nature of social development is still quite vaguely understood and confusing, particularly where children are concerned.

While it is relatively easy to identify certain components of physical fitness, such as strength, endurance and the like, this is not necessarily the case with components of social fitness. The components of physical fitness are the same for children as for adults. The components of social fitness for children, on the other hand, may differ from those for adults. By some adult standards children might be considered social misfits, since some of their behavior might not be socially acceptable to some adults.

To the chagrin of some adults, young children are uninhibited in their social development. In this regard, we need to be concerned with social maturity as it pertains to the growing and ever-changing child. This is to say that we need to give consideration to certain characteristics of social maturity and how well they are dealt with at the different stages of child development.

Perhaps adults should ask themselves such questions as: Are we helping children to become self-reliant by giving them independence at the proper time? Are we helping them to be outgoing and interested in others as well as themselves? Are we helping them to know how to satisfy their own needs in a socially desirable way? Are we helping them to develop a wholesome attitude toward themselves and others?

Guidelines for Social Development Through Dance

Guidelines for social development are set forth here in the same manner that guidelines for physical development through dance were proposed in the previous discussion; that is, these guidelines take the form of valid *concepts of social development*. When we have some basis for understanding the social behavior of children as they grow and develop, we will then be in a better position to select and conduct dance activities that are compatible with social development. The following list of concepts of social development with their implications for dance is submitted with this general idea in mind.

1. *Interpersonal relationships are based on social needs.* All children should be given an equal opportunity in dance participation. Moreover, the teacher should impress upon children their importance to the group. This can be done in connection with the group effort in a particular dance, which is so essential to successful participation.

2. *A child can develop his or her self-concept through undertaking roles.* A child is more likely to be aware of his or her particular abilities if given the opportunity to take different parts in a dance. Rotation of such responsibilities tends to provide opportunity for self-expression of children through role-playing.

3. *There are various degrees of interaction between individuals and groups.* The dance experience should provide an outstanding setting for the child to develop interpersonal interaction. The teacher has the opportunity to observe children in dance movement situations

rather than in merely sedentary situations. Consequently, the teacher is in a good position to guide integrative experiences by helping children to see the importance of satisfactory interrelationships in a dance situation.

4. *Choosing and being chosen—an expression of a basic need—is a foundation of interpersonal relationships.* As often as possible, children should be given the opportunity to choose partners in dances that require this. However, great caution should be taken by the teacher to see that this is carried out in an equitable way. The teacher should devise methods of choice such that certain children are not always selected last or left out entirely.

5. *Language is a basic means and essential accompaniment of socialization.* Children can be taught the language of the body through using the names of its parts as they participate in a dance. This is an important dimension in the development of body awareness. Dance experiences should be such that there is opportunity for verbal expression among and between children. For example, in the evaluation phase of a dance lesson, children have a fine opportunity for meaningful oral expression if the evaluation is skillfully guided by the teacher.

6. *Learning to play roles is a process of social development.* A child should be given the opportunity to play as many roles as possible in the dance experience. This could include being involved in the organization and administration of dance activities, such as selection of activities and helping others with dance skills. Exercising a physical skill is in itself the playing of a role, such as being a better dancer. Thus, the very medium of dance is the process of social adjustment.

7. *Integrative interaction tends to promote social development.* The key word in this process of promoting development is *action*, which is the basis for dance. Dance is unique in its potential for accomplishing integrative interaction and thus for promoting social development. Spontaneity can be considered one of the desired outcomes of integrative experiences; providing the opportunity for actions and feelings expressed by the child as he or she really is. Movement is perhaps the most important aspect of life for

young children, and thus spontaneous actions and feelings are best expressed through activity.

8. *Resistance to domination is an active attempt to maintain one's integrity.* The teacher might well regard child resistance as a possible indicator of teacher domination. If this occurs the teacher should look into his or her own actions, which may be dominating the teaching–learning situation. Child resistance should be interpreted as a sign of a healthy personality, and a wise teacher will be able to direct the energy into constructive channels to promote social development. A very natural outlet for this frustrated energy is found in desirable activities presented in the dance program.

9. *Interpersonal interaction between children is a basis for choice.* If children are left out by other children, this symptom should be studied with care to see whether this indicates poor interpersonal relationships with other children. Very interesting aspects of interpersonal relationships can be observed by the wise teacher. Children may realize the value of a child's contribution to a specific activity and accept such a child accordingly. On the other hand, they may be likely to accept their friends regardless of ability in dance skills.

10. *A child, in and as a result of belonging to a group, develops differently than he or she can as an individual alone.* Many dance activities provide an outstanding opportunity for children to engage actively in a variety of group experiences. Merely being a member of a group can be a most rewarding experience for a child. If properly conducted, dance activities should provide an optimal situation for desirable social development, because children focus their greatest personal interest in movement experiences.

What Should Dance Do for Children Socially?

The elementary school dance "laboratory" should present ideal surroundings for the social development of children. In fact, it is doubtful whether any other laboratory has greater potential to operate on the basis of democratic principles. Cooperating for the benefit of the entire group, meeting the other children and the teacher on a more or less informal basis, and other social factors inherent in dance are important in helping each individual child become a socially accepted member of the group. It must be borne in mind, however, that the social values to be derived from dance will not necessarily accrue automatically. For example, there is some objective evidence indicating that children who perform physical skills most proficiently are most popular with other children. It therefore should follow that if each child has the opportunity to develop optimum ability, he or she should have greater opportunity for social acceptance among his or her peers.

Although the area of dance presents a setting for an ideal social environment, at the same time there are situations in which children are likely to suffer social rejection. For example, open methods of selecting partners for certain types of dances by pupil choice can possibly result in situations where someone must be selected last, and sometimes reluctantly, by his or her group. In addition, faulty grouping of children for dance can result in a kind of social ostracism because one child may not "keep time" as well as others. These factors as well as others must be taken into consideration by the teacher in dance program planning if the best social values are to be obtained.

EMOTIONAL DEVELOPMENT

In considering the subject of emotion, we are confronted with the fact that this is a difficult concept to define, and that for years, ideas and theories in the study of emotion have been continually changing.

It is not the purpose here to attempt to go into any great depth on a subject that has long represented one of the most intricate challenges in the field of psychology. A few general statements relative to the nature of emotion do appear to be in order, however, if we are to understand more clearly how it might be concerned with dance.

Emotion could be described as *a response one's body makes to a stimulus for which it is not prepared, or which suggests a possible source of gain or loss.* For example, if a child is confronted with a situation and does not have a satisfactory response, the emotional pattern of fear may result. If one finds himself or herself in a position where desires are frustrated, the emotional pattern of anger may occur.

This line of thought suggests that emotions might be classified in two ways: those that are pleasant and those that are unpleasant. Joy, for instance, is a pleasant emotional experience, while fear is an unpleasant one. It is interesting to note that a good portion of the literature is devoted to emotions that are unpleasant. One finds that psychology books give much more space to such emotional patterns as fear, hate, guilt, and anxiety than to such pleasant emotions as love, sympathy, and contentment.

Generally speaking, the pleasantness or unpleasantness of an emotion seems to be determined by its strength or intensity, by the nature of the situation arousing it, and by the way an individual perceives or interprets the situation. The emotions of young children tend to be more intense than those of adults. If an adult is not aware of this aspect of child behavior, he or she will be unlikely to understand why a child may react rather violently to a situation that an adult would consider insignificant. The fact that different individuals will react differently to the same type of situation should also be taken into account. For example, something that might anger one child might have little influence on another.

Guidelines for Emotional Development Through Dance

Guidelines for emotional development are given here in the same way that guidelines for physical and social development through dance were proposed in the previous discussions; that is, these guidelines take the form of valid *concepts of emotional development.* When we have a basis for the emotional behavior of children as they grow and develop, we are in a better position to provide dance experiences that are compatible with emotional development. The following list of concepts of emotional development with their implications for dance is submitted with this general idea in mind.

1. *An emotional response may be brought about by a goal's being furthered*

or thwarted. The teacher should make a very serious effort to assure successful dance experiences for every child. This can be accomplished in part by attempting to provide for individual differences within given dance experiences. The dance setting should be such that each child derives a feeling of personal worth through making some sort of positive contribution.

2. *Self-realization experiences should be constructive.* The opportunity for creative experience inherent in dance affords the child an excellent opportunity for self-realization through physical expression. Teachers might consider planning with children themselves in order to see to it that the activities meet their needs, and thus, provide a constructive experience.

3. *Emotional responses increase as the development of the child brings greater awareness, the ability to remember the past and to anticipate the future.* The teacher can remind the children of their past emotional responses with words of praise. This should encourage children to repeat such responses in future similar dance situations, and thus make for a better learning situation.

4. *As the child develops, the emotional reactions tend to become less violent and more discriminating.* A well-planned program and progressive sequence of dance activities can provide for release of aggression in a socially acceptable manner.

5. *Emotional reactions displayed in early childhood are more likely to continue in some form in later years.* This could be one of the best reasons for providing dance experiences for children. Through dance experiences in the formative years we can help children develop constructive emotional reactions through the medium that they understand best—movement. Through the freedom to express emotional reactions spontaneously in the dance experience, the real feelings of the child are more easily identified.

6. *Emotional reactions tend to increase beyond normal expectancy toward the constructive or destructive on the balance of furthering or hindering experiences of the child.* For some children, the confidence they need to be able to face the problems of life may be acquired through physical expression. Therefore, dance has tremendous potential to help contribute toward a solid base of total development.

5. *Depending on certain factors, a child may accept or reject his or her own feelings.* Children's dance experiences should make them feel good and have confidence in themselves. Satisfactory self-concept is closely related to body control; therefore, dance experiences might be considered one of the best ways of contributing to it.

What Should Dance Do for Children Emotionally?

We are aware of the fact that all children manifest emotional behavior as well as ordinary behavior. Differences in the organic structure and in the environment of children will largely govern the degree to which the individual child expresses emotional behavior.

There appears to be one very outstanding way in which dance experiences can help to make the child more secure and emotionally stable: Dance is a means of releasing aggression in a socially acceptable manner. Indeed, the very atmosphere that should prevail in the dance situation, a happy situation free from stress and fear, promotes a feeling of emotional well-being.

INTELLECTUAL DEVELOPMENT

The word "intelligence" is derived from the Latin word *intellectus,* which literally means the "power of knowing." Intelligence has been defined in many ways. One general description of it is *the capacity to learn or understand.*

Children possess varying degrees of intelligence, most falling within a range of what is called "normal." In dealing with this form of development we should perhaps try to determine the components of intellectual fitness. However, this is difficult to do. Because of the somewhat vague definition of intelligence it is practically impossible to identify specific components of it. Thus, we need to view intellectual fitness in a somewhat different manner.

For purposes of this discussion I will therefore consider intellectual fitness from two different but closely related points of view: first, from the standpoint of intellectual needs, and second, from the standpoint of how certain things influence intelligence. If the child's intellectual needs are being met, perhaps we could also say, from the first point of view, that he or she is intellectually fit. From the second point of view, if we know how certain things influence intelligence, we might understand better how to contribute to intellectual fitness by improving the quality of these influential factors.

There appears to be rather general agreement with regard to the intellectual needs of children. Among others, these needs include (1) a need for challenging experiences at the child's level of ability, (2) a need for intellectually successful and satisfying experiences, (3) a need for the opportunity to solve problems, and (4) a need for the opportunity to participate in creative experiences instead of always having to conform.

Some of the factors that tend to influence intelligence are (1) health and physical condition, (2) emotional disturbance, and (3) certain social and economic factors. When teachers understand intellectual needs and factors influencing intelligence, perhaps they will be able to deal more satisfactorily with children to help them in their intellectual pursuits. As just mentioned, an important intellectual need for children is the opportunity to participate in creative experiences. This need is singled out for special mention because the opportunities for creative experiences are perhaps more inherent in the dance situation than many other aspects of the elementary school curriculum.

Guidelines for Intellectual Development Through Dance

Again these guidelines take the form of valid *concepts of intellectual development*. When we have some sort of basis for understanding the intellectual behavior of children as they grow and develop, we are then in a better position to provide dance experiences that are compatible with intellectual development. The following list of concepts of intellectual development with implications for dance is submitted with this general idea in mind.

1. *Children differ in intelligence.* Teachers should be aware that the poor performance of some children in dance activities might be due to

the fact that they have difficulty with communication. Differences in intelligence levels as well as in physical skill and ability need to be taken into account in the planning of dance lessons.

2. *Mental development is rapid in early childhood and slows down later.* Children want and need challenging kinds of dance experiences. Dance lessons should be planned and taught in much the same way as other subjects of the curriculum.

3. *Intelligence develops through the interaction of the child and his environment.* Movement experiences in dance involve a process of interaction with the environment. There are many problem-solving opportunities in the well-planned dance environoment, and thus the child can be presented with challenging learning situations.

4. *Emotional stress may affect measures of intelligence.* Dance experiences have potential value in the relief of emotional stress. This can make the child more effective intellectually.

5. *Extremes in intelligence show differences in personality characteristics.* The teacher should be aware of the range of intelligence of children in a particular group. Experiences should be provided that challenge the so-called gifted child as well as meeting the needs of those children who are below average. In the dance experience children can learn about how to respect individual differences as far as levels of intelligence are concerned.

6. *The child's self-concept of his ability to deal with intellectual tasks influences his successful dealing with such tasks.* The dance experiences should contain a degree of variation. This way it is more likely to insure that all children will achieve success at one time or another.

7. *Situations that encourage total development appear to provide the situations for intellectual development.* The potential for total development is likely to be more evident in dance than in some other areas of the curriculum. If one were to analyze each of the subject areas according to its potentialities for physical, social, emotional, and intellectual development, it is doubtful that many of these areas would surpass the potential inherent in the dance learning situation.

What Should Dance Do for Children Intellectually?

Close scrutiny of the possibilities of intellectual development through dance reveals that a very desirable contribution can be made through this medium. This belief is substantiated in part by the affirmations made by such eminent philosophers and educators as Plato, Locke, Rousseau, Pestalozzi, and numerous others. Plato's postulation that learning could take place better through play, Locke's thoughts on a sound mind and sound body, Rousseau's belief that all children should receive plenty of wholesome physical activity early in life, and Pestalozzi's observations that children approach their studies with a greater amount of interest after engaging in enjoyable physical activity, have all contributed to the modern idea that dance and intellectual development are closely associated.

With regard to the last-mentioned theorist, Johann Heinrich Pestalozzi (1746–1827), it has been suggested that this famous Swiss educator laid the foundation for modern teaching. He is considered one of the great pioneers in stressing the importance of child study as a basis for helping children learn. While observing his own child, Pestalozzi noticed that after playing for a time the boy tended to concentrate on his studies for an unusually long period.

In a well-taught dance lesson there are numerous opportunities for children to exercise judgment and resort to reflective thinking in the solution of various kinds of problems. Moreover, some of my own research has indicated that dance activities provide a desirable learning medium for the development of concepts in other subject areas of the elementary school curriculum. (Chapters 10 and 11 will discuss some of these possibilities in more detail.)

EMERGENCE OF DEVELOPMENTAL OBJECTIVES OF DANCE FOR CHILDREN

The elements of total development can satisfactorily emerge as valid dance objectives for children. These elements have been expressed in terms of physical, social, emotional, and intellectual development.

As such they can logically become the physical, social, emotional, and intellectual objectives of dance for children.

The term *objective* appears to have been adopted by education from the military. The latter uses it to identify areas to be assaulted and/or captured in some way. The *Dictionary of Education* gives the following definition of the term as *aim, end in view, or purpose of a course of action or a belief; that which is anticipated as desirable in the early phases of an activity and serves to select, regulate, and direct later aspects of the act so that the total process is designed and integrated.*[3] Various other terms, such as *aim, goal,* and *purpose,* are used to convey the same meaning. Whatever term is used, we might well consider it in relation to a very simple question, i.e., what should the dance objectives imply where total development of children is concerned? With this in mind, consider the following.

The Physical Objective

This objective should imply the development of skill and ability in a variety of dance activities, together with organic development commensurate with vigor, vitality, strength, balance, flexibility, and neuromuscular coordination.

The Social Objective

This objective should imply satisfactory experiences in how to meet and get along with others, development of proper attitudes toward one's peers, and the development of a sense of values.

The Emotional Objective

This objective should imply that sympathetic guidance should be provided in meeting anxieties, joys, and sorrows, and help given in developing aspirations, affections, and security.

---

[3] Carter, Good, *Dictionary of Education,* 2nd ed. (New York: McGraw-Hill, 1959), p. 371.

The Intellectual Objective

This objective should imply the development of specific knowledge about a variety of worthwhile dance learning experiences. In addition, this objective should be concerned with the value of dance as a most worthwhile learning medium in the development of concepts and understandings in other areas of the curriculum.

CHAPTER 3

TEACHING AND LEARNING IN DANCE FOR CHILDREN

THE TEACHER

The most important aspect of any teaching–learning situation is the child (learner). However, attention is most often paid to the teacher. Frequently, a communication medium appears that is heralded not only as a teaching aid, but even a teacher substitute. The enormous expense of mass education, coupled with the need for high-quality teaching, has given rise to the wish that somehow a relatively few master teachers could direct the learning of large numbers of students. In this way, it has been reasoned, both the quantitative and the qualitative problems of American education could be solved or at least minimized.

Several of the mass media of communication have been proposed with varying degree of enthusiasm as the answer to this problem of educating large numbers of children well. Recordings, radio, films, television, teaching machines, and other mechanical and technical devices have been experimented with and widely used. In spite of their great value in education, all the mass media of communication have been found wanting when tried as teacher "substitutes" rather

33

than as teaching "aids," perhaps especially at the elementary school level. It is interesting to consider why.

In brief, the answer probably lies in the fact that although a teacher usually deals with a group of children, he or she must remain sensitive to the individual. The qualified teacher is aware that every child is unique and that he or she approaches all learning tasks with his or her own level of motivation, capacity, experience, and vitality. Moreover, such a teacher is aware that the individuals in a class must be prepared for a learning experience in order that the experience may in some way be recognized by them as having meaning for them. Preparation of any class must be made in terms of the particular individuals in that class. The teacher must then, by a combination of emotional and logical appeal, help each individual find his way through the experience at his own rate and, to some extent, in his own way. The teacher must also help the individual "nail down" the meaning of the experience to himself and help him to incorporate it and its use into his own life. The point of view reflected here is that there is no substitute for the competent teacher who, while necessarily teaching a group, is highly sensitive to the individual children involved. The "teacher" who expects a group of children to learn adequately through the use of a mere recording to provide instructions for a dance is grossly negligent in his or her duty.

The role of the teacher in providing dance learning experiences for children differs little from that in other teaching–learning situations. The essential difference is that the teacher deals with the children in movement experiences, while in the other subject matter areas the learning activities are more or less sedentary in nature.

The teacher's role should be that of a guide who supervises and directs desirable dance learning experiences. In providing such experiences the teacher should constantly keep in mind how dance can contribute to the physical, social, emotional, and intellectual development of every child. This implies that the teacher should develop an understanding of the principles of learning and attempt to apply these principles properly in the teaching of dance. (These principles will be discussed in detail later in the chapter).

It is important that the teacher recognize that individual differences exist among teachers as well as children and that some of these differences will influence their teaching methods. Sometimes one teacher may have greater success than another with a particular method. This implies that there should be no specific, resolute method of teaching for all teachers. On the other hand, teachers should allow themselves to deviate from recommended conformity if they are able to provide desirable learning experiences through a method peculiar to their own abilities. This, of course, means that the procedures used should be compatible with conditions under which learning takes place best.

TEACHING AND LEARNING

The teaching–learning process is complicated and complex. For this reason it is important that teachers have as full an understanding as possible of the role of teaching and learning in dance for children.

Basic Considerations

The concepts of learning that an individual teacher or a group of teachers in a given school subscribe to are directly related to the kind and variety of dance learning activities and experiences that will be provided for children. Because of this it is important for teachers to explore some of the factors that make for the most desirable and worthwhile learning. Among the factors that should help to orient the reader toward some basic understandings in the teaching of dance are (1) the meaning of certain terms, (2) the derivation of teaching methods, and (3) the various learning products in dance.

Meaning of Terms

Due to the fact that certain terms, because of their multiple use, do not actually have a universal defintion, no attempt will be made here to define terms. On the other hand, it will be the purpose here to describe certain terms rather than to attempt to define them. The reader should view the descriptions of terms that follow with this general idea in mind.

Learning. The term learning has already been described in Chapter 1 as involving some sort of change in the individual.

Teaching. Several years ago I was addressing a group of teachers on the subject of teaching and learning. Introducing the subject in somewhat abstract terms, I asked, "What is teaching?" After a short period of embarrassing deliberation, one member of the group ventured the following answer, with some degree of uncertainty: "Is it imparting information?" This kind of thinking is characteristic of the traditional understanding of the term "teaching." A more acceptable description of teaching would be drawn in terms of guidance, direction, and supervision of behavior that results in desirable and worthwhile learning. This is to say that it is the job of the teacher to guide the child's learning rather than to impart to him or her a series of unrelated and sometimes meaningless facts.

Method. The term "method" might be regarded as an orderly and systematic means of achieving an objective. In other words, method is concerned with "how to do" something in order to achieve desired results. If best results are to be obtained for children through dance, it becomes necessary that the most desirable dance learning experiences be provided. Consequently, it becomes essential that teachers use all of the ingenuity and resourcefulness at their command in the proper direction and guidance of these learning experiences. The procedures that teachers use are known as *teaching methods.*

Derivation of Teaching Methods

Beginning teachers often ask, "Where do we get out ideas for teaching methods?" For the most part this question should be considered in general terms. In other words, although various acceptable teaching procedures are utilized in the modern school, all these methods are likely to be derived from two somewhat broad sources.

The first of these is the accumulated knowledge of educational psychology and what is known about the learning process in providing dance learning experiences. The other is the practice of successful teachers.

In most instances, the undergraduate preparation of prospective teachers includes at least some study of educational psychology as it applies to the learning process and certain accepted principles of learning. With this basic information it is expected that beginning teachers have sufficient knowledge to apply to the practical situation.

It has been my observation over a period of years that many beginning teachers tend to rely too much upon the practices of successful teachers as a source of teaching methods. The validity of this procedure rests on the assumption that such successful practices are based on fundamental psychological principles of learning. Nevertheless, it should be the responsibility of every teacher to become directly familiar with these psychological principles and to attempt to apply them in the best possible way to children's dance.

Learning Products in Dance

In general, three kinds of learning products accrue from participation in dance activities, namely, direct, incidental, and indirect. In a well-planned program these learning products should develop satisfactorily through dance activities.

Direct learning products are those that are the direct object of teaching. For instance, basic dance movements contain some of the important skills necessary for reasonable degrees of proficiency in certain dances. Through the learning of dance skills in the form of basic dance movements, more enjoyment is derived from participating in a dance activity than would be gained from the mere practice of the skills. For this reason the learning of dance skills is one of the primary direct objects of teaching. However, it should be understood that certain incidental and indirect learning products can result from direct teaching in dance. The zeal of a participant to become a more proficient performer gives rise to certain incidental learning products. These may be inherent in the realization and acceptance of practices of healthful living, which make the individual a more skilled performer in the activity.

Attitudes are often at the root of behavior tendencies, and as such might well be concerned with indirect learning products. This type of learning product involves such qualities as appreciation of certain aspects of dance and other factors that involve the adjustment and modification of the individual's reactions to others.

Teachers who have the responsibility for providing dance programs for children—physical education teachers, music teachers, classroom teachers, or special dance teachers—should give a great deal of consideration to these various kinds of learning products. This is particularly important if children are to receive the full benefit of the many dance learning experiences that should be provided for them.

SOME PRINCIPLES OF LEARNING APPLIED TO DANCE

There are various basic facts about the nature of human beings of which modern educators are more cognizant than educators of the past. Essentially, these facts involve some of the fundamental aspects of the learning process, which all good teaching should take into account. Older concepts of teaching methods were based largely upon the idea that the teacher was the sole authority in terms of what was best for children, and that children were expected to learn regardless of the conditions surrounding the learning situation. For the most part, modern teaching replaces the older concepts with methods that are based on certain accepted beliefs of educational psychology. Outgrowths of these beliefs emerge in the form of principles of learning. The following principles provide important guidelines for arranging learning experiences for children, and they suggest how desirable learning can take place when these principles are satisfactorily applied to dance.

1. *The child's own purposeful goals should guide his learning activities.* In order for a desirable learning situation to prevail, teachers must consider certain features of the purposeful goals which guide learning activities. Of utmost importance is the fact that the goal must seem worthwhile to the child. This will perhaps involve such factors as interest, attention, and motivation. Fortunately, in the recommended activities from which dance learning experiences are drawn, interest, attention, and motivation are likely to be inherent qualities. Thus, it is not always necessary for the teacher to "arouse" the child with

various kinds of motivating situations. Having said that, I should mention that it can be profitable in a given teaching–learning situation to "slip in" a form of extrinsic motivation.

I might refer to a case from my own experience. In this particular instance I had become aware of a difficulty in getting boys and girls to choose partners with each other in some of the activities in which they had been participating. This was particularly true as I began to introduce certain dance activities. On one particular occasion I began the class as follows:

> TEACHER: Boys and girls, when reading about sports events in the paper the other day, I came across some sentences that I thought would be of interest to you. In a story about a football game, one sentence said, 'The halfback danced down the field." In another report there was a sentence that said, 'The runner danced back and forth off of first base.' As I thought about this, it occurred to me that dancing might be a good way to develop some of the skills needed to play well in sports and games. Have any of you ever heard of how dancing could help make better players?
>
> FIRST BOY: Gee, I never thought of it that way before.
>
> SECOND BOY: Me, either.

Of course, the intent was not to suggest that dance should have to "lean on" other kinds of activities to be accepted. On the contrary, the purpose was to try to show an association and compatible relationship of one particular kind of activity (dance) to another (sports and games).

In any event, the goal should not be too difficult for the child to achieve. Although it should present a challenge, it should be something that is commensurate with a child's abilities and within the realm of achievement. By the same token the goal should not be too easy or it will not be likely that the child will have the opportunity to develop to his greatest possible capacity. To be purposeful, a goal should give direction to activity and learning. In substance, this implies that after a child has accepted a goal he should have a better idea of where he is going and what he should be able to accomplish in a given situation.

It is important that the child find, adopt, and accept his own goals. This implies that he should not receive them directly from the teacher. If the most desirable kind of learning is to take place, it is doubtful whether one person can give another person a goal. This should not be interpreted to mean that goals may not originate with the teacher. The teacher can be of considerable help in assisting children to find their own goals. This can be done by planning the dance learning environment in such a way that children with varying interests and abilities may find something that appears to be worthwhile. This procedure can be followed and still be in keeping with the teacher's objectives. For instance, it may be a goal of the teacher to improve the social relationships of children in a given dance class. This might be accomplished by providing a variety of dance activities that involve frequent change of partners. Experience has shown that this procedure has been most useful in welding together a group of children who have previously experienced some difficulty in getting along together. Although the goal of obtaining better social relationships originated with the teacher, the experience was planned in such a way that the goal was eventually adopted by the children.

2. *The child should be given sufficient freedom to create his own responses in the situation he faces.* This principle indicates that *problem solving* is a very important means of human learning, and that to a large extent the child will learn only through experience, either direct or indirect. This implies that the teacher should provide every opportunity for children to utilize judgment in the various situations that arise in dance activities.

It should be borne in mind that although the child learns through experience, this does not mean that experience will assure desirable learning, since it might possibly come too soon. For example, children at the first-grade level should not be expected to learn some of the complex dance patterns, simply because at that level they may not be ready for it.

When children are free to create their own responses in the situation they face, individual differences are being taken into consideration, and, generally, experience comes at the right time for desirable learning. This situation necessitates an activity-area environment flexible enough to allow children to achieve in relation to their individual abilities.

In a sense, this principle of learning refutes, and perhaps rightly so, the idea that there is a specific "problem-solving method" mutually exclusive from other methods. In other words, all methods should involve problem solving, which actually means the application of this principle.

3. *The child agrees to and acts upon the learning which he considers of most value to him.* Children accept as most valuable those things that are of greatest value to *them*. This principle implies in part, then, that there should be a satisfactory balance between the *needs* and the *interests* of children as criteria for the selection of dance activities. Although it is of extreme importance to consider the needs of children in developing experiences, the teacher should not lose sight of the fact that their interest is needed if the most desirable learning is to take place.

Although needs and interests of children may be closely related, there are nevertheless differences that should be taken into consideration when dance learning activities are selected. Interests are mostly acquired as products of the environment, while needs, particularly those of an individual nature, are more likely to be innate. Herein lies one of the main differences in the two criteria insofar as concerns the selection of dance learning activities. For instance, a child may demonstrate a temporary interest in an activity that may not contribute to his or her needs at a certain age level. This interest may be aroused because of the child's environment. Perhaps an older brother, sister, or a parent may influence a child to develop an interest in an activity that would not contribute to his needs, or that would possibly have a detrimental effect on him. Despite the inevitability of such contingencies, interests of children may serve as one of the valid criteria for the selection of dance learning activities. In this connection it is interesting to note that there is a rather marked relationship between dance learning activities recommended by teachers and child interest in these same activities.

To a certain extent interests may be dependent upon past experiences of children. For instance, interests in certain dance activities may stem from the fact that they are a part of the traditional background of the community and as such have absorbed the interest of parents as well as children. (Needs and interests of children will be discussed in greater detail in Chapter 5).

4. *The child should be given the opportunity to share cooperatively in learning experiences with his or her classmates under the guidance, but not the complete control of the teacher.* The point that should be emphasized here is that although learning may be an individual matter, it is likely to take place best in a group. This is to say that children learn individually, but that socialization should be retained. Moreover, sharing in group activities seem absolutely essential in educating for democracy.

The dance situation should present near-ideal conditions for a desirable balance between individualization and socialization. For example, the elements of an activity such as certain dance steps and movements are learned individually, but then they are combined by the entire group in a dance situation.

5. *The teacher should act as a guide who understands the child as a growing organism.* This principle indicates that the teacher should consider learning as an evolving process and not just as instantaneous behavior. If teaching is to be regarded as the guidance and direction of behavior which results in learning, the teacher must display wisdom as to when to "step in and teach" and when to step aside and watch for further opportunities to guide and direct behavior.

The application of this principle precludes an approach of teacher domination. On the other hand, the implementation of this principle is perhaps more likely to be realized in dance classes where the teacher recognizes that numerous problem-solving situations are inherent in many dance situations. For example if a particular dance activity is not going as it should, the teacher can stop the activity and evaluate it with the children so that they can determine how the activity may be improved. In other words, children are placed in a position to identify problems connected with the activity and given the opportunity to exercise judgment in solving them. The teacher thus helps the children discover direct pathways to meaningful areas of experience and at the same time contributes to the children's ability to become self-directed individuals.

PHASES OF THE TEACHING–LEARNING SITUATION

There are certain fundamental phases involved in almost every dance teaching–learning situation. These are (1) auditory input, (2) visual input, (3) participation, and (4) evaluation. Although these four phases are likely to be weighted in various degrees, they will occur in the teaching of practically every dance lesson regardless of the type of activity that is being taught. Although the application of the various phases may be of a general nature, they nevertheless should be utilized in such a way that they become specific in a particular situation. Depending upon the type of dance activity being taught, the use and application of the various phases should be characterized by flexibility and awareness of the objectives of the lesson.

Auditory-Input Phase

The term *auditory* may be described as stimulation occurring through the sense organs of hearing. In education the term *input* is concerned with the use of as many media as are deemed necessary for a particular teaching–learning situation. The term *output* is concerned with behaviors or reactions of the learner resulting from the various forms of input. Auditory input involves the various learning media that are directed to the auditory sense. This should not be interpreted to mean that the auditory-input phase of the teaching–learning situation is a one-way process. Although much of such input may originate with the teacher, consideration should also be given to verbal interaction among children and between the children and the teacher.

Dance provides a most desirable opportunity for learning through direct purposeful experience. In other words, the dance learning situation is "learning by doing," or learning through pleasurable physical activity. Although verbalization might well be kept to a minimum, a certain amount of auditory input, which should provide for auditory-motor association, appears to be essential for a satisfactory teaching–learning situation. The quality of "kinesthetic feel" may be described as the process of changing ideas into muscular action, and is of primary importance in the proper acquisition of dance skills. It might be said that the auditory-input phase of teaching helps to set the stage for a kinesthetic concept of the particular activity being taught.

Listening experiences are, no doubt, among the most abstract of the learning media used with children. As such, this type of learning experience has been much maligned by some educators. However it should be pointed out that the child first learns to act on the basis of verbal instructions by others. In this regard, it has been suggested that later on he learns to guide and direct his own behavior on the basis of his language activities; he literally talks to himself and gives himself directions.

This point of view is supported by research, which has postulated that speech as a form of communication between children and adults later becomes a means of organizing the child's own behavior. The function that was previously divided between two people—child and adult—later becomes an internal function of human behavior.

Great care should be taken with the auditory-input phase in the dance teaching-learning situation. The ensuing discussions are intended to suggest to the reader ways in which the greatest benefits can accrue when using this particular learning medium.

Preparing the Children for Listening

Since it is likely that the initial part of the auditory-input phase will originate with the teacher either through verbalization or musical accompaniment, care should be taken to prepare the children for listening. The teacher may set the scene for listening by relating the activity to the interest of the children. In addition, the teacher should be on the alert to help children develop their own purposes for listening.

In preparing children to listen, the teacher should be aware that it is important to consider the comfort of the children, and that attempts should be made to remove any possible attention-distracting factors. Although evidence concerning the effect of environmental distractions on listening effectiveness is not in great abundance, there is reason to believe that distraction does interfere with listening comprehension. Moreover, it was reported years ago that being able to see as well as hear the speaker is an important factor in the prevention of listening distraction.

These factors have a variety of implications for the auditory-input phase of the dance teaching–learning situation. For example, consideration should be given to the placement of children when a dance activity requires auditory input from the teacher. This means, for instance, that if the teacher is providing auditory input from a circle formation, the teacher should take a position as a part of the circle instead of speaking from the center of the circle. With reference to the listener being able to see the speaker, teachers might exercise caution in the use of records for dance activities that include instructions on the record. Particularly with primary level children it might be well for the teacher to use the instructions only for himself or herself and the musical accompaniment for the children.

Teacher–Child and Child–Child Interaction

It was mentioned previously that the auditory-input phase is a two-way process. As such, it is important to take into account certain factors involving verbal interaction of children with children, and teacher with children.

By "democracy" some people seem to mean that everyone ought to do or say whatever happens to cross his mind at the moment. This raises the question of control, and it should be emphasized that group discussions, if they are to be democratic, must be kept under control. This is to say that if a group discussion is to succeed there must be control, and I would stress that democracy implies discipline and control.

Group discussion is a kind of socio-intellectual exercise (involving numerous bodily movements, of course) just as basketball is a kind of socio-intellectual exercise (involving, too, higher mental functioning). Both imply individual discipline to keep play moving within bounds, and both require moderators (or officials) overseeing, though not participating in, the play in a manner that is objective and aloof from the heat of competition. In brief, disciplined, controlled group discussion can be a training ground for living in a society in which both individual and group interests are profoundly respected.

Another important function of teacher–child interaction is with the time given to questions after the teacher has provided auditory input. The teacher should give time for questions from the group, but should be very skillful in the use of questions. It must be determined immediately whether or not a question is a legitimate one. This implies that the type of questions asked can help to serve as criteria for the teacher to evaluate the auditory-input phase of teaching. For example, if numerous questions are asked, it is apparent that either the auditory input from the teacher was unsatisfactory or that children were not paying attention.

Directionality of Sound

In summarizing recent findings concerned with the directionality of sound, one finds a number of interesting factors important to the auditory-input phase emerging. Individuals tend to initiate movements toward the direction from which the sound cue emanates. For example, if a verbal cue is given that instructs the individual to move a body segment or segments to the left, but the verbal cue emanates from the right side of the individual, the initial motor response is to the right, followed by a reverse response to the left. To underscore the importance of this, it is recommended that when working on direction of motor responses with children one should make certain that sound cues come from the direction in which the motor response is to be made. The point is made that children have enough difficulty in discriminating left from right without confusing them further.

Visual-Input Phase

The term *visual* is concerned with images that are obtained through the eyes. Thus, visual input involves the various learning media that are directed to the visual sense.

Various estimates indicate that the visual sense brings us upwards of three-fourths of our knowledge. If this postulation can be used as a valid criterion, the merits of the visual-input phase in dance teaching are readily discernible. In many cases visual input, which should provide for visual-motor association, serves as a happy medium between verbal symbols and direct participation, thus helping teachers further to prepare children for the kinesthetic feel mentioned previously. In general, there are two types of visual input that can be used satisfactorily in teaching dance. These are visual symbols and human demonstration (live performance).

Visual Symbols

Included among the visual symbols that may be used in dance are motion pictures and various kinds of flat or still pictures. One of the disadvantagesd of the latter centers around the difficulty of portraying movement by means of a still figure. Although movement is obtained with a motion picture, it is not projected in a third dimension, which causes some degree of ineffectiveness when this medium is used.

Human Demonstration

The following are some guides to action in the use of human demonstration:

1. If the teacher plans to demonstrate, this should be included in the preparation of the lesson by practicing and rehearsing the demonstration.
2. The teacher does not need to do all the demonstrating; in fact, in many cases it may be much more effective to have one or more children demonstrate. Since the teacher is expected to be a skilled

performer, a demonstration by a child will oftentimes serve to show other children that one of their peers can perform the activity and that they should be able to do it also.

3. A demonstration should be based on the skill and ability of a given group of children. If it appears to be too difficult for them, they might not want to attempt the activity.

4. When at all possible, a demonstration should parallel the timing and conditions which will prevail when it is put to practical application. However, if the situation is one in which the movements are complex or done with great speed, it might be well to have the demonstration conducted more slowly than would be the case in the actual performance situation.

5. The group should be arranged so that everyone is in a favorable position to see the demonstration. Moreover, the children should be able to view the demonstration from a position where it takes place. For example, if the dance is to be performed in a lateral plane, children should be placed so that they can see it from this position.

6. Although auditory input and human demonstration can be satisfactorily combined in many situations, care should be taken that auditory input is not lost, because the visual sense offsets the auditory sense; that is, one should not become an attention-distracting factor for the other. It will be up to the teacher to determine the amount of verbalization that should accompany the demonstration.

7. After the demonstration has been presented it may be a good practice to demonstrate again and have the children go through the movements with the demonstrator. This provides for the use of the kinesthetic sense together with the visual sense that makes for close integration of these two sensory stimuli.

Participation Phase

Direct purposeful experience is the foundation of all education. Because dance activities are motor in character, there is a near-ideal situation for learning in this particular area of the curriculum. The child needs to be involved in a dance in order to gain a full appreciation of it. There is an opportunity in a well-taught dance lesson for learning to become a part of the child's physical reality, providing for a pleasurable concrete experience rather than an abstract one. For this reason the following considerations should be kept in mind in connection with the participation phase of teaching.

1. The class period should be planned so that the greatest possible amount of time is given to participation.
2. If the activity does not progress as expected in the participation phase, perhaps the fault may lie in the procedures used in the auditory- and visual-input phases. Participation then becomes a criterion for the evaluation of former phases.
3. The teacher should take into account the need for initial attempts in learning an activity to meet with a reasonable degree of success.
4. The teacher should constantly be aware of the possibility of fatigue during participation and should understand that individual differences in children give rise to variation in the rapidity with which fatigue sets in.
5. Participation should be worthwhile for every child, and all children should have the opportunity to achieve. Dances which call for elimination of participants should be avoided lest some individuals fail to receive the full value from participation.
6. The teacher should be ever on the alert to guide and direct learning, thus making the dance period a teaching–learning period.
7. During the participation phase, the teacher should constantly analyze the children's performance in order to identify those who need improvement. Behavior of children should be observed while they are engaging in dance activities. For example, various types of emotional behavior might be noted in dance situations that might not be indicated in any other school activity.
8. Problems involved during participation should be kept in mind for subsequent evaluation of the lesson with the children.

Evaluation Phase

Evaluation, although a very important phase of the dance teaching–learning situation, is nevertheless, perhaps, one of its most neglected aspects. For instance, it is not uncommon for the class period to end at the signal of a bell, the children hurrying and scurrying from the activity area without having participated in an evaluation of the results of the lesson.

Children should be given the opportunity to discuss the lesson and to suggest ways in which improvement might be effected. When this procedure is followed, children are placed in a problem-solving situation and desirable learning is more likely, with the teacher guiding learning rather than dominating the situation by giving directions. Also, more and better continuity from one lesson to another is likely to result when time is taken for evaluation. In addition, children are much more likely to develop a clearer understanding of the purposes of dance if they are given an opportunity to discuss the procedures involved in the lesson.

Ordinarily, the evaluation phase should take place at the end of the lesson. Experience has shown that a satisfactory evaluation procedure can be effected in three to six minutes, depending upon the nature of the activity and what actually occurred during a given lesson. Under certain circumstances, if an activity is not proceeding well in the participation phase, it may be desirable to stop the activity and carry out what is known as a "spot" evaluation. This does not mean that the teacher should stop an activity every time the situation is failing to develop according to plan. A suggestion or a hint to those children who are having difficulty with performance can perhaps make it unnecessary for all the children to cease participation. On the other hand, if the situation is such that the needs of the group can best be met by discussing the problem, the teacher is indeed justified in stopping the activity and conducting an evaluation "on the spot."

Teachers should guard against stereotyping the evaluation phase of the dance lesson. This implies that the teacher should look for developments during the participation phase of the lesson that might well serve as criteria for evaluation at the end. If the evaluation phase is always initiated with the question "Did you like it?" this part of the lesson will soon become meaningless and merely time-consuming for the children. Depending upon what actually occurred during the participation phase, the following general questions might be considered by the teacher when beginning the evaluation phase with the children:

1. Should we review briefly what we learned today?
2. What are some of the things we learned today?
3. What do we have to do or know in order to be a good performer in this dance?
4. What did today's activity do for our bodies? Did it help us to have better control over our feet and legs? Did you find that you had to breathe much faster when you danced?
5. What were some of the things you liked about the dancing we did today?
6. Can you think of any ways that we might improve the dance we learned today?

Questions such as these place children in a problem-solving situation and consequently provide for a more satisfactory learning situation. Moreover, this procedure is likely to provide a better setting for a child-oriented dance lesson, because children have an opportunity to discuss together ways and means to improve the performance of the activities.

A very important feature of the evaluation phase is that the teacher has an opportunity to evaluate teaching procedures with a given group of children. In other words, the teacher should have a better understanding of how well the lesson was taught when able to hear at first-hand the impressions of the children who participated.

PLANNING DANCE LESSONS

The *lesson plan* is a statement of desired achievements, together with the means by which these are to be attained as a result of the dance activities participated in during a specified time that a group spends with the teacher.

The success of any dance program will depend to a large extent upon the daily dance experiences of children. This implies that lessons in dance should be as carefully planned as in other areas of the curriculum.

Dance lesson planning should take into account those factors that indirectly and directly influence the teaching–learning situation. This means that the teacher must consider class organization as a very important factor when daily lessons are planned, because various conditions associated with it can have an indirect influence on the dance learning situation. For example, it will be desirable for the teacher to effect a plan of class organization that (1) is conducive to carrying out the objectives of the lesson, (2) provides enough activity for each child, and (3) provides for the best use of facilities. After sufficient consideration has been given to ways and means of class organization in developing the dance lesson, the teacher should take into account the essential characteristic features that directly influence the teaching–learning situation. In this regard, it is strongly emphasized that teachers might well devise their own lesson outlines or patterns. This appears to be essential if teachers are to profit from the flexibility inherent in a plan that fits their own needs. With this idea in mind, the following lesson plan outline, indicating some of the features that might be incorporated into a dance plan, is submitted as a guide for the reader.

1. *Objectives.* A statement of goals that the teacher would like to see realized during the lesson.
2. *Content.* A statement of the dance learning activities in which the class will engage during the lesson.
3. *Class procedures.* A brief account of procedures to be followed in conducting the lesson, such as (a) techniques for initiating interest and relating previous teaching–learning situations to the present lesson, (b) auditory input, (c) visual input, (d) participation, and (e) evaluation.
4. *Teaching materials.* A statement of essential materials needed for the lesson.

If the teacher is to provide dance learning experiences that contribute satisfactorily to the total development of children, there must be a clear perspective of the total learning that is expected from dance. This total learning requires a progression in dance activities, which in turn necessitates some means of preserving continuity from one class period to another. Consequently, each individual lesson must become a link in the chain of dance learnings that contribute to the total development of the child. Experience has shown that the implementation of this theory can be most successfully accomplished by wise and careful lesson planning.

TEACHING RESPONSIBILITY

It seems appropriate to end this chapter with some statements about where to place the responsibility for providing desirable dance learning experiences. There does not appear to be "one best plan" of teaching that fits all conditions. At the present time most of the responsibility is given to the physical education teacher, when such a person is available. Regardless of efforts to provide a specific area of dance in the elementary school curriculum and a special teacher of dance, physical education teachers are likely to continue to have the major responsibility. (The reader should refer back to Chapter 1 on the survey of teaching responsibility).

Traditionally, dance activities have been classed as one of three broad areas of the physical education curriculum—the others being games and gymnastic activities. At present, my surveys show that on average about 20 percent of the physical education time is allotted to dance at the primary level and about 15 percent at the intermediate level. This contrasts with one of my studies about 25 years ago that indicated that some schools were allotting as much as 60 percent of the total physical education time to dance activities at the primary level and 40 percent at the intermediate level. The reasons for this difference at the present time may be that some physical education teachers, especially men, are reluctant to teach dance activities, and that more time is being devoted to sports skills. Another reason in some cases may be that parents as well as educators feel that dance should be a part of the child's out-of-school experience. Since this raises questions as to the validity of dance, teachers should exert their influence to show its value as an area of the school curriculum.

Another carrier of responsibility is the regular classroom teacher. Many postulations have been made with regard to the classroom teacher and the special teacher as to which of them is in the better position to provide dance learning experiences. It is well known that some individuals are staunch proponents of the use of either the classroom teacher or the special teacher exclusively. It is also recognized that various arguments can be set forth which purport to show how any one plan is more effective than others.

Contemporary thought indicates that the classroom teacher and special teacher should be mutually involved. The special teacher and the classroom teacher need to pool and share their knowledge and abilities so that the most worthwhile learning experiences can be provided for children through dance.

In summary, there are a few general considerations that should be taken into account. The specific way of designating the responsibility for teaching will depend upon a number of factors. Among others, these include: (1) the underlying philosophy of the local school, (2) preparation, experience, and interest of personnel, (3) facilities and time allotment for dance, and (4) funds available for implementation of the program.

In the final analysis the teaching plan employed must be compatible with the local situation and, above all, one that meets the needs of all of the children satisfactorily. For this reason it seems essential that all factors pertinent to local conditions be thoroughly appraised and evaluated before a particular plan of teaching is introduced. Moreover, any plan should be subjected to continuous evaluation so that desirable practices can be retained or modified and undesirable practices eliminated as the occasions demands.

CHAPTER 4

BRANCHES OF DANCE FOR CHILDREN

In the mid-1970s I introduced a classification which divided the broad area of physical activity into three different branches. The arbitrary terminology used to identify these branches was *curricular* physical activity, *cognitive* physical activity, and *compensatory* physical activity. In more recent years I have applied this concept to specific areas of physical activity—in the present case, *dance:* thus, curricular dance, cognitive dance, and compensatory dance.

Although each branch is conceived as a separate entity, there is obvious overlapping among them, since the basic and underlying concept in the utilization of dance experiences is the same in any situation: These experiences are all oriented in various degrees to the physical, social, emotional, and intellectual development of children. With this idea in mind the various branches are described in the following discussions.

CURRICULAR DANCE

Curricular dance is the branch with which most readers will probably be most familiar. It implies that dance should be a curriculum area in the same way as mathematics or science. Such factors as sufficient facilities, adequate time allotment, and above all, good teaching, should be provided to carry out the most desirable dance learning experiences for children.

A dance curriculum that is child-oriented and scientifically developed should be provided, as would be the case for the language arts curriculum or the social studies curriculum or any other curriculum in the school. It is in this branch that the child should learn to move efficiently and effectively and to learn the various kinds of dance skills. Curricular dance includes all manner of dance activities and it is important that a variety of these be provided for children. For example, the National Dance Association Task Force on Dance for Children has recommended experiences that involve such diversified dance areas as basic locomotor movements, creative dance, movement songs, and ethnic and folk dances. Many of these experiences will be presented in Chapters 6, 7, and 8 of this volume. (In view of the fact that most readers will be much less familiar with the concepts of cognitive and compensatory dance, these branches will be dealt with in detail in the discussions to follow).

COGNITIVE DANCE

This branch of dance for children, which considers its use as a learning medium in other curriculum areas, might well be considered a relatively recent innovation. In essence, the procedure involves the selection of a dance activity which embodies to a relatively high degree some specific skill or concept from a given subject area. This dance activity is taught to the children and used as a learning activity to develop that skill or concept.

The Theory of Cognitive Dance

The important role of pleasurable movement in cognition and learning has been recognized for centuries. Throughout the ages, some of the most profound thinkers in history have noted the value of pleasurable physical activity as a way of learning.

The cognitive dance learning medium addresses the problem of how children can develop skills and concepts in other school subject areas while actively engaged in certain kinds of dance activities. Although children differ in various characteristics, the fact remains that they share certain general similarities. One common feature of children is that they all move. Cognitive dance is based essentially on the theory that children will learn better when what we might call "academic learning" takes place through pleasurable physical activity—in this case in the form of some aspect of dance. As mentioned previously, the procedure for learning through dance involves the selection of a dance activity which is then taught to the children and used as a learning activity in the development of a skill or concept of a specific subject area. An attempt is made to arrange an active learning situation so that a fundamental skill or concept is being practiced in the course of participating in the dance activity. Activities are selected on the basis of the degree of inherence of a skill or concept in a given school subject area, as well as the appropriate physical ability and social level of a given group of children.

Essentially, there are two general types of such activities. One type is useful for developing a specific concept, where the learner "acts out," and is thus able to visualize as well as to get the "feel" of the concept. Concepts become a part of the child's physical reality as the child participates in the activity in which this concept is inherent. An example of such an activity involving the study of fractions follows.

This is a structured dance to the accompaniment of "Pop Goes the Weasel." Groups of three children, with hands joined, form a small circle. These groups are arranged in a large circle as in the following diagram (see page 60).

Each group walks around counterclockwise until the strain "Pop Goes the Weasel" is heard on the recording (See Recording Source No. 7). At this time one child is "popped" under the joined hands of the other two and sent to the next couple in the large circle. Progression of those "popped" is counterclockwise. Before starting the dance, it must be decided which person in each group will be "popped" through, and the sequence in which the other two will be "popped" through.

This example is depicted in a *simulated teaching–learning* situation:

TEACHER: Please form a large circle with a boy and girl in every other place (*Children form the circle*). Today we are going to learn a dance called "Pop Goes the Weasel." Probably some of you have heard the tune before. How many have? (*Some children indicate that they are familiar with the tune*). Do you remember the other day when we were studying fractions, what we said the bottom number told us?

CHILD: I think it was how many parts something is divided into.

TEACHER: Yes, that's right, and now we are going to divide our large circle into groups of three. Starting here, we will form small circles with three persons in each small circle with hands joined. (Teacher and children demonstrate with first group of three to her left). Now each group is a circle made up of three persons. If something is divided into three parts, what do we call the name of each part?

CHILD: One-third?

TEACHER: Yes, that's right. Can someone tell us how many thirds make a whole?

CHILD: Three?

CHILD: (Aside to another child) Oh! I see now what she meant the other day.

TEACHER: All right. Now, let's have each person in the small circles take the name of either, First-Third, Second-Third, or Last-Third. Just take a little time to decide within your own circle who will take each part. (*Teacher and children demonstrate with one of the small circles*). Let me see the hands of all the First-Thirds, the Second-Thirds, and the Last-Thirds. Now here is something that is very important. The magic word in this dance is "Pop." That is if the words to the tune were to be sung. We will move to the right in our own circles. When we come to the part of the music where the word "Pop" would be sung, the person in each circle with the name First-Third will pop under the arms of the other two persons in his circle and become a part of the circle on the right. The people in the small circles will immediately begin to walk again, and this time on the word "Pop" the person named Second-Third will leave his circle and will become a part of the circle on his right. The people in the small circles will immediately begin to walk again, and this time on the word "Pop" the person named Second-Third will leave his circle. The next time the person named Last-Third leaves. Who do you think will pop next time?

CHILD: Would we start all over again with First-Third?

TEACHER: Yes, that's right, and we will continue that way until the record has finished playing. I am going to play a part of the record for you. This time I want you to listen to the music, and when you hear the part where you pop into the next circle raise your hand so that we can make sure that you will know when to pop. That's fine. Everyone seems to know when to pop. Listen for the chord to start.

(*Children participate in the dance, and after the record is played through once, the teacher evaluates the activity with them.*)

TEACHER: What were some of the things you noticed that you thought were good about our first attempt at this dance?

CHILD: We all seemed to go in the right direction and didn't get mixed up.

CHILD: We kept time pretty well.

TEACHER: What are some of the things you like about it?

CHILD: I liked always being in a different circle.

CHILD: Well it made me catch on to the fractions better.

CHILD: Me too. We ought to do arithmetic that way all the time.

TEACHER: You think it was easier to learn fractions that way?

CHILD: I'll say, and it was lots more fun.

TEACHER: What are some of the ways we might improve it if we tried it another time?

CHILD: We ought to try to all pop at the same time.

CHILD: Maybe we shouldn't try to go around the circle so fast.

TEACHER: Yes, those are good suggestions. Personally, I think it was rather well done for our first attempt.

The second type of activity helps to develop skills by using these skills in highly interesting and stimulating situations. Repetitive drill for the development of skills related to specific concepts can be utilized. An example of this type of activity follows.

This dance activity requires a minimum of five participants, who stand in a circle. One child is *It*. He walks around inside the circle. As the players sing the following song, to the tune of "Twinkle, Twinkle, Little Star," they act out the words of the movement song.

Take away, take away, take away one.
Come with me and have some fun.
Take away, take away, take away two.
Come with me, oh yes please do.
Take away, take away, take away three.
All please come and skip with me.

It taps one person. This person follows behind *It*. *It* then taps a second and third person. At the end of the song all three persons try to get back to their places in the circle. *It* also tries to get into one of the vacant places. The remaining person can be *It* for next time.

This activity enables a child to see demonstrated the concept of subtraction. The teacher may have a child identify how many persons are left each time *It* takes away one person.

A very important precautionary measure with regard to cognitive dance should be mentioned at this point; that is, this approach should be considered as only "one" aspect of dance and not the major purpose of it. We should consider dance as a curriculum area in its own right, as with curricular dance, discussed above. Consequently, the use of dance as a learning medium for other subject areas should not ordinarily occur during the regular time allotted to dance. On the contrary, this approach should be considered a learning activity in the same way that other kinds of learning activities are used in a given curriculum area. This means that, for the most part, cognitive dance should be used during the time allotted to the particular curriculum area in question. Moreover, the classroom teacher would ordinarily do the teaching when this approach is used. The function of the special teacher would be to work closely with the classroom teacher and to furnish him or her with suitable dance activities to use in the development of concepts.

Factors Influencing Learning Through Cognitive Dance

During the early school years, and from ages six to eight in particular, limits to learning may frequently be imposed by a relatively short attention span rather than by intellectual capabilities alone. Some children who do not appear to think or learn well in abstract terms can more easily grasp concepts when given an opportunity to use them in an applied manner. In view of the fact that children are creatures of movement and also that they are likely to deal better in concrete than in abstract terms, it would seem to follow naturally that the dance learning medium is well suited to them.

By this I should not be interpreted as suggesting that learning through dance movement experiences (motor learning) and passive learning experiences (verbal learning) are two different kinds of learning. The position is taken here that "learning is learning," even though in the dance approach the motor component may be operating at a higher level than in most of the traditional types of learning activities.

The theory of learning accepted here is that learning takes place through reorganization of the systems of perception into a functional and integrated whole as the result of certain stimuli. As previously stated, this implies that problem-solving is a most desirable means of human learning and that learning takes place well through prroblem solving. In a well-planned dance learning situation, a great deal of consideration should be given to the inherent possibilities for learning in terms of problem solving. In fact, most dance lessons offer abundant opportunities for near ideal teaching–learning situations because of the many problems to be solved.

Another important factor to consider with respect to dance as a learning medium is that much of the learning in young children is movement-oriented, and that the child devotes a good proportion of his attention to locomotor activity. Furthermore, learnings of a motor nature tend to usurp a large amount of the young child's time and energy and are often closely associated with other learnings. In addition, it is recognized by experienced teachers at the primary grade levels that the chlid's motor mechanism is so active that it is almost impossible for him to remain in a quiet state for very long, even in the passive learning situation.

To demand that children stay seated for long periods of time actually goes against a basic physiological principle directly related to the child's basal metabolism. The term *metabolism* refers to physical and chemical changes in the body involving the production and consumption of energy. The rate at which these physical and chemical processes are carried on when the individual is in a state of rest represents his *basal metabolism*. Thus, the basal metabolic rate indicates the speed at which body fuel is changed to energy, as well as how fast this energy is used.

Basal metabolic rate can be measured in terms of calories per meter of body surface, with a calorie representing a unit measure of heat energy in food. It has been found that, on the average, basal metabolism rises from birth to about two or three years of age, at which time it starts to decline until the ages of 20 to 24. Also, the rate is higher for boys than for girls. With the highest metabolic rate and therefore, the greatest amount of energy occurring during the early school years, deep consideration should be given to learning activities through which this energy can be utilized. Moreover, it has been observed that primary-age children show an increased attention span during pleasurable physical activity. When a task such as a dance experience is meaningful to a child, he or she can spend longer periods engaged in it than is likely to be the case with some of the more traditional types of learning activities.

In the comments made thus far I have alluded to some general aspects of the value of cognitive dance. The ensuing discussions will focus more specifically upon what I call certain *inherent facilitative factors* in the dance learning medium which are highly compatible with child learning. These factors are (1) *motivation,* (2) *proprioception* and (3) *reinforcement,* all of which are somewhat interdependent and interrelated.

Motivation

With regard to motivation as an inherent facilitative factor of learning through the dance medium, I like to think of it as an application of incentives to arouse interest in order to get a child to perform in a desired way.

I would also distinguish between extrinsic and intrinsic motivation. Extrinsic motivation can be described as the application of incentives external to a given activity in order to make work palatable and to faciliate performance, while intrinsic motivation is the determination of behavior that is inherent in an activity and sustains it, as with autonomous acts and interests.

Extrinsic motivation has been and continues to be used as a means of spurring individuals to achievement. This most often takes the form of various kinds of reward incentives. The main objection to this type of motivation is that it tends to focus the learner's attention upon the reward rather than the learning task and the total learning situation.

In general, the child is motivated when he or she discovers what seems to be a suitable reason for engaging in a certain activity. The most valid reason, of course, is that the child sees a purpose for the activity and derives enjoyment from it. Children must feel that what they are doing is important and purposeful. When this occurs, and the child gets the impression that he or she is achieving success in the group situation, motivation is intrinsic, since it comes about naturally as a result of the child's interest in the activity. It is the premise here that cognitive dance contains this "built-in" ingredient so necessary to desirable and worthwhile learning.

The ensuing discussions of this section of the chapter will be concerned with two aspects of motivation that are considered to be inherent in the dance experience. These are (1) motivation in relation to *interest,* and (2) motivation in relation to *knowledge of results.*

Motivation in relation to interest. It is important to understand the meaning of interest and to appreciate how interests function as an adjunct to learning. *Interest* is a state of being in relation to some object which excites one's special attention. *Interests* are such objects themselves when constantly maintained.

A condition for learning is a situation in which a child agrees with and acts upon the learnings that he or she considers of most value. (This was previously stated as a principle of learning). To many children their dance experiences are of personal value.

Under most circumstances a very high interest level is shown in dance situations simply because of the pleasure children tend to expect from such activities. The structure of a learning activity is directly related to the length of time the learning can be tolerated by the learner without loss of interest. Dance experiences by their very nature are more likely to be so structured than many of the traditional learning activities.

Motivation in relation to knowledge of results. Knowledge of results is most commonly referred to as *feedback.* It was suggested many years ago that feedback is the process of providing the learner with information as to how accurate his reactions were.

Many psychologists feel that knowledge of results is the strongest, most important variable controlling performance and learning, and, further, that studies have repeatedly shown that there is no improvement without it, progressive improvement with it, and deterioration after its withdrawal. As a matter of fact, there appears to be sufficient objective evidence to indicate that learning is usually more effective when one receives some immediate information as to how one is progressing. It would appear rather obvious that such knowledge of results is an important adjunct to learning, because without it one would have little idea as to which responses were correct.

Cognitive dance provides almost instantaneous knowledge of results because the child can actually *feel* what he or she has done. The child does not become the victim of a poorly constructed paper and pencil test, the results of which may have little or no meaning to him.

Proprioception

Earlier in this chapter it was stated that learning, according to the theory accepted here, takes place through a reorganization of the systems of perception into a functional and integrated whole as a result of certain stimuli. These systems of perception, or sensory processes as they are sometimes referred to, are ordinarily considered to consist of the senses of sight, hearing, touch, smell, and taste. Although this point of view is convenient for some purposes, it greatly oversimplifies the ways in which information can be fed into the human organism; that is, it overlooks a number of sources of sensory input, particularly the senses that enable the body to maintain its correct posture. As a matter of fact, the 60 to 70 pounds of muscles, over 600 in number, attached to the skeleton of the average-sized man could well be his most important sense organ.

Various estimates indicate that the visual sense brings us upwards of three-fourths of our knowledge. Therefore, it could be said with little reservation that man is "eye-minded." It has been reported, however, that a larger portion of the nervous system is devoted to receiving and integrating sensory input originating in the muscles and joint structures than is devoted to the eye and ear combined. In view of this, it could be contended that man is "muscle-sense" minded.

Generally speaking, *proprioception* is concerned with muscle sense. The proprioceptors are sensory nerve terminals that give information concerning movements and positions of the body. A proprioceptive feedback mechanism, in a sense, regulates movement. In view of the fact that children are so movement oriented, it appears reasonable to speculate that proprioceptive feedback from the receptors of muscles, skin, and joints contributes in a facilitative manner when the dance learning medium is used to develop academic skills and concepts. The combination of the psychological factor of motivation and the physiological factor of proprioception, inherent in the dance learning medium, has caused me to coin the term mot*or*vation to describe this phenomenon.

Reinforcement

In considering the compatibility of the dance learning medium with reinforcement theory, the meaning of reinforcement needs to be taken into account. An acceptable general description of reinforcement would be that there is *an increase in the efficiency of a response to a stimulus brought about by the concurrent action of another stimulus.* The basis for contending that the dance learning medium is consistent with general reinforcement theory is that this medium reinforces attention to the learning task and learning behavior. It keeps children involved in the learning activity, which is the major area of application for reinforcement procedures. Moreover, there is perhaps little in the way of human behavior that is not reinforced, or at least reinforcible by feedback of some sort, and the importance of proprioceptive feedback has already been discussed in this particular connection.

To summarize this discussion, it would appear that the dance learning medium generally establishes a more effective situation for learning reinforcement for the following reasons:

1. The greater motivation of children in the dance learning situation involves accentuation of those behaviors directly pertinent to their learning activities, making these salient for the purpose of reinforcement.

2. The proprioceptive emphasis in the dance learning medium involves a greater number of *responses* associated with and conditioned to learning stimuli.
3. The gratifying aspects of dance situations provide a generalized situation of *reinforcers.*

Although it is difficult to predict what the future holds for cognitive dance, I feel assured that more serious attention will be increasingly paid to it. Discussions with leading neurophysiologists, learning theorists, child-development specialists, and others reveal a positive feeling toward the dance medium of learning; and there is general agreement that the premise is very sound from all standpoints: philosophical, physiological, and psychological.

COMPENSATORY DANCE

The term *compensatory* as it applies to education is not new, and over the years it has been used in a variety of ways. Possibly its derivation dates back to mid-nineteenth century Denmark.[1] At that time what was knovn as the "compensatory education of cripples" involved the teaching of boys and young men with certain physical impairments such skills as basketmaking and shoemaking. The purpose was to prepare people who had certain deformities to be able to make a living on their own.

In this country at about the turn of the century it was reported that, "by compensatory education for deformed children is meant any special training which will make amends for their physical shortcomings and convert little cripples into men and women better fitted in some one direction to cope with fellow-man in the struggle for life."[2]

In recent years in this country, compensatory education has taken on a much different meaning; it has been concerned essentially with "compensating" for an inadequate earlier education in some way, or

[1] "The Education of Crippled Children," *American Physical Education Review,* 3, No. 3 (September 1898), pp. 190–191.
[2] Ibid.

with providing a better background for beginning school children who come from a low socio-economic background. A case in point is the "Headstart" program sponsored by the federal government.

Educators and psychologists in Great Britain have attached still a different meaning to compensatory education. In this regard, it is indicated that the term *compensatory education* now being used tends to replace the former term *re-education*. It is contended that the term re-education was often misused when standing for compensatory education. Re-education implied educating again persons who had previously reached an adequate educational level and who now for some reason did not exhibit behavior at a level of which they were previously capable. Thus, compensatory education implies an attempt to make good a deficiency in a person's earlier education. Examples of this are some of the structured *perceptual-motor training* programs that have originated in the United States.

It is from the British source that I have derived the term *compensatory dance*. The rationale for this term is that ordinarily the attempts to improve a deficiency in one's earlier education are likely to take place through the physical aspect of the individual's personality—in this case dance. Whereas the standard structured perceptual-motor training programs purport to improve learning ability through systematic exercises and procedures, compensatory dance, as perceived here, seeks to improve upon learning ability through participation in regular dance activities.

Although compensatory dance and cognitive dance are based on essentially the same concept, the manner in which these two approaches are used should not be confused. It could be said that compensatory dance is essentially concerned with education *of* the physical, while cognitive dance is concerned with education *through* the physical.

Compensatory dance attempts to correct various types of child learning disabilities which may stem from an impairment of the central nervous system and/or have their roots in certain social or emotional problems of children. This branch of dance, most often through the medium of *perceptual-motor development*, involves the correction, or at least some degree of improvement, of certain motor deficiencies, especially those associated with fine coordination. What some specialists have identified as a "perceptual-motor deficit" syndrome is said to exist with certain neurologically handicapped children. An attempt may be made to correct or improve fine motor control problems through a carefully developed sequence of motor competencies that follow a definite hierarchy of development. This may occur either through the structured perceptual-motor program, which is likely to depend upon a series of systematic physical exercises, or through compensatory dance, which attempts to provide for these corrections or improvements by having children engage in dance activities based upon perceptual-motor developmental factors. This procedure tends to be much more fun for children and at the same time it is more likely to be free from emotionally traumatizing situations which may arise in some structured perceptual-motor programs.

The advantage of compensatory dance is that it can be incorporated into the regular dance program rather easily. It can be a part of the function of the teacher responsible for dance, and, with assistance, the classroom teacher can handle many aspects of compensatory dance.

The foregoing statements should not be interpreted as an extensive criticism of structured perceptual-motor programs. Under certain conditions, and perhaps particularly in cases of severe neurological dysfunction, such programs can be useful. However, caution and restraint in the use of highly structured perceptual-motor training should be exercised, and these programs should be conducted under adequate supervision and by properly prepared personnel.

Children Who Can Benefit from Compensatory Dance

We need to identify the type of child who can receive the most satisfactory benefits from compensatory dance. Ordinarily, those children who have certain problems in learning are placed in the broad category of *slow learners*. One classification of slow learners is (1) children with mental retardation, (2) children with depressed potential, and (3) children with learning disabilities. It is this third group—children who have learning disabilities—with which compensatory dance is most vitally concerned. (The final chapter of the book will detail numerous compensatory dance activities).

Since classroom achievement of children with learning disbilities and of those who suffer from mental retardation or depressed potential may be similar, the problem of identification is of utmost importance. Many times the child with a learning disability is thought of as slow or lazy when in reality he is neither. These labels can have an adverse effect on future learning, on self-perception, and on feelings of personal worth.

Research on the identification of children with learning disabilities indicates that while their achievement has been impaired in specific areas of both verbal and/or nonverbal learning, their potential for learning is nevertheless categorized as normal or above. Thus, these children with learning disabilities fall within the IQ range of 90 and above in either the verbal or nonverbal areas. Total IQ is not used as the criterion for determining learning potential. This is because adequate intelligence (either verbal or nonverbal) may be obscured in cases where the total IQ falls below 90 even though specific aspects of intelligence are adequate. The child whose IQ falls below the normal range and who has a learning disability is considered to have a multiple involvement.

A child with a learning disability has deficits in verbal and/or nonverbal learning. There may be impairment of expressive, receptive, or integrative functions. There is concern for deficits in the function of input and output, of sensory modalities and overloading, and of degree of impairment. The essential differences between the mentally retarded person and the person with a learning disability were characterized as long as two decades ago follows:

> One cannot deny that the neurology of learning has been disturbed in the mentally retarded, but the fundamental effect has been to reduce potential for learning in general. Though some retarded children have isolated *high* levels of function, the pattern is one of generalized inferiority; normal potential for learning is *not* assumed. In comparison, children with learning disabilities have isolated *low* levels of function. The pattern is

one of generalized integrity of mental capacity; normal potential *is* assumed.[3]

Consequently, the child with a learning disability shows marked differences from the child with limited potential. There are both qualitative and quantitative differences. This child has more potential for learning, and the means by which he or she learns are different.

Although there may be some overlapping in the educational methods used with the groups identified as slow learners, there obviously must be differentiation in educational goals and approaches for these various groups. Correct identification of the factors causing slowness in learning is essential in teaching to the individual differences of children. The theories and practices labeled as compensatory dance outline an effective approach for teachers working with the child appropriately identified as one with learning disabilities.

It appears logical to assume that dance activities can be a very important medium in perceptual-motor development. Perhaps for many children a very successful type to use would be creative dance, where the child responds by expressing himself according to how the rhythmical accompaniment makes him feel. When the child is able to use his body freely, there is a strong likelihood of increased body awareness. Creative dance will also give the child free self-direction in space, as well as self-control, in that he is not involved with a partner as in a more structured dance activity. In this regard it should be mentioned, however, that there is also merit in some cases in performing the activity within the framework of an established pattern. This is particularly true as far as emotional release is concerned. Mental hygienists know that some persons can express themselves with more spontaneity in a relatively structured situation than in one where they have more freedom. Such persons, when they skip, dance, clap, and whirl to the rhythm of the music may be expressing themselves with an abandon that is not possible when they are left free to express themselves in any way at all.

Over the years these theoretical postulations have been borne out

[3] D. J. Johnson, and H. R. Myklebust, *Learning Disabilities,* (New York: Grune, 1967), p. 55.

by research. For example, in the area of neurological dysfunctioning in the visual-perceptual-auditory areas, disabled readers are frequently found to lack coordination in such basic motor movements as walking and running. And further, motor *rhythm* is often lacking in children with reading, writing, and spelling problems. Improvement of this motor rhythm tends toward alleviating these deficiencies. It has also been found that dyslexic children who are given training in fine motor skills, such as handwriting, and pattern motor skills—especially folk dancing—show improvement in reading. (In the final chapter I will discuss in detail how certain dance activities can improve the child's body awareness, laterality, and directionality, as well as the various forms of perception).

CHAPTER 5

DEVELOPING THE DANCE CURRICULUM FOR CHILDREN

Since there has been some confusion with regard to the term *curriculum*, it seems essential to describe at the outset of this chapter what it means. The word curriculum has been employed in a number of different ways over the years, and the result has been a misunderstanding as to just what it actually entails.

In the past the curriculum has in some instances been confused with the course of study, and as a result these two terms have been used interchangeably. It should be understood, however, that the concept of curriculum is very broad in scope and that the course of study is actually an outgrowth of curriculum development.

For some time now, the curriculum as it pertains to elementary education has been considered to include all school experiences that in one way or another influence the child. Of course these experiences should be guided, supervised, and directed in such a way that they are channeled toward the achievement of the objectives of the elementary school.

In order to keep pace with current advanced thinking in the whole area of education, teachers of dance should no doubt accept this broad concept of curriculum. This is particularly important since there are so many facets and ramifications that must combine in order to make a program of dance satisfactory. Moreover, a variety of factors in one way or another tend to influence the elementary school dance curriculum. Because the scope of dance differs somewhat from other areas in the elementary school, it is necessary to identify some of the things upon which a successful elementary school dance program may depend. Such factors as (1) the attitude of school administrators, (2) facilities and equipment, (3) teaching responsibility, and (4) time allotment all affect the status that dance may have in a particular elementary school.

Because of these influencing factors it is exceedingly difficult to expect much uniformity in dance programs among schools. Hence some educators have tended to take a more or less dim view of dance because of its lack of standardized curriculum content in relation to other areas. It should be understood, however, that a fair comparison cannot be made with the standardized curriculum content of other subject areas, because the aforementioned influencing factors have tended to preclude any comparable standardization of the dance curriculum content.

Although there may be lack of standardization in specific dance curriculum content from one elementary school to another, this should not imply that dance will not contribute to the total purpose of the elementary school. Teachers in one school may be meeting objectives through one group of dance activities while those in another school may be meeting objectives through other dance activities.

SOME BASIC PRINCIPLES OF DANCE CURRICULUM DEVELOPMENT

It is essential that those responsible for dance curriculum development take into consideration certain guides to action. Where dance programs have developed on a more or less haphazard basis, it is likely that they could be improved to some extent through sound principles of curriculum development.

The list of principles suggested here is not necessarily all-inclusive, nor is each principle a separate entity. It may be noticed that they overlap to some extent and, as a consequence, serve the purpose of the basic considerations essential to the success of the dance program.

1. *Dance curriculum development should be based on a philosophy of equal opportunity for all children.* Dance is the rightful heritage of all children in all schools. If principles of democracy are to be practiced in the schools of America, dance programs must be devised so that all children will have an equal opportunity to engage in wholesome activity.

2. *Dance curriculum development should utilize all available appropriate resources.* Those persons responsible for curriculum development should survey each resource and evaluate its possible use in the program. Such factors as multiple use of facilities and wise placement of teaching personnel must be given consideration in curriculum development for the betterment of the program.

3. *Dance curriculum development should be a cooperative enterprise.* It does not seem wise to place the development of the curriculum in the hands of a single individual. Supervisors, teachers, and others, possibly parents and children, should share their knowledge and experience in an attempt to develop a program that will make a significant contribution to the optimum growth and development of children.

4. *Learning activities and experiences in the dance curriculum should be selected through the application of valid criteria.* Although there may perhaps be little in the way of objective scientific evidence to support the placement of dance activities at the various age and grade levels, there are nevertheless certain criteria sufficiently valid to justify their application.

5. *Dance curriculum development should recognize individual differences in children.* In order to develop each individual to his or her ultimate capacity, dance curriculum development needs to take into consideration the fact that children differ in physical ability as well as social, emotional, and intellectual characteristics. Such factors as organization of classes and classification of children must be regarded as highly significant if the school plans to assume the responsibility for the optimum development of each child.

6. *Dance curriculum development should be flexible.* The lack of standardization in the dance curriculum makes it almost imperative that it be characterized by a degree of flexibility. Varying backgrounds of previous child experiences in various dance forms together with such factors as wide differences in facilities from school to school manifest the need for a curriculum that can be adapted to meet the specific needs of the children of a particular school.

7. *Dance curriculum development should be continuous.* Since education is considered a continuous process, it naturally follows that dance curriculum development, in order to meet the needs of a changing society, should be continuous.

THE PROBLEM OF GRADE PLACEMENT OF DANCE LEARNING EXPERIENCES

Suitable grade placement of dance learning experiences presents a problem for teachers because of the lack of objective scientific evidence to support the selection of activities for the various age levels. In the past, the activities that have been suggested for children of the various age levels have been based for the most part upon experiences of dance educators as well as physical educators, and to some extent upon past traditions. Although it can be rationalized that either of these criteria may be valid, depending upon circumstances, other valid criteria should be explored for the proper grade placement of dance learning experiences.

Until such time as more sufficient objective evidence is available to support the placement of dance activities at specific grade levels, teachers and others must resort to experience, along with their knowledge of the principles of child growth and development, in order to provide desirable, worthwhile dance learning experiences for all children. Teachers therefore needs to develop basic understandings of growth and developmental traits and characteristics of children. (In a subsequent section of the chapter I will deal in detail with this subject).

Almost three decades ago I made the following recommendation with regard to grade placement of dance learning experiences:

One of the most desirable mediums for child expression through movement is found in dance and rhythmic activities. One need look only to the function of the human body to see the importance of rhythm in the life of the child. The heart beats in rhythm, the digestive processes function in rhythm, breathing is done in rhythm; in fact, almost anything in which human beings are involved is done in a more or less rhythmic pattern.

At the primary level, fundamental rhythmic activities found in the locomotor movements of walking, running, jumping, hopping, leaping and galloping and the nonlocomotor or axial movements, such as twisting, turning and stretching form the basis of skills for all types of dance patterns. Creative dance helps children to express themselves in just the way the accompaniment "makes them feel" and gives vent to expression so necessary in the life of the child. Other activities suitable for use at the primary level include, among others, folk dances and singing games.

Children at the upper elementary level, if they have had a sufficient background of dance and rhythmic activities at the primary level, enjoy activities such as more complicated forms of folk dancing, play-party games and mixers, square dancing, and social dancing.[1]

In this general regard it is interesting to note some of the grade placement recommendations of the National Dance Association Task Force. Following are some selected statements from the Task Force report set forth in the previously mentioned publication *Children's Dance:*

1. The Guidelines attempt to cover recommended dance activities for children from the ages of 3 to 12. This span of years is divided into those of early childhood (3–7 years) and those of middle childhood (8–12 years). While many activities are appropriate for all ages if there is adaptation by the teacher to the level of development,

[1] James H. Humphrey, *Elementary School Physical Education,* (New York, Harper, 1958), pp. 48–49.

there are nevertheless a few which serve their purpose best with either younger or older children (p. 7).

2. *Singing Movement Songs*—Inclusion in comprehensive dance curriculum of 'learned' dances which help to motivate movement in early childhood, such as action or movement songs, singing games, or song dances (p. 9).

3. For *middle childhood years:* Using Folk Dances—Opportunity for quick learning and dancing with fun and satisfaction of traditional folk dances if based on earlier learnings (p. 9).

An analysis of the preceding comments would appear to indicate that recommendations for grade placement of dance learning experiences have not changed appreciably over time. Of course, there still remains the need to identify valid criteria for selection of dance curriculum content.

CRITERIA FOR THE SELECTION OF DANCE CURRICULUM CONTENT

It is of utmost importance that valid criteria be applied in the selection of dance learning activities and experiences. In this regard, the two most basic criteria are the *needs* and *interests* of children. (Some of the comments made previously about needs and interests will be reiterated in the following discussion for purposes of continuity).

Needs of Children

In their efforts to develop a sound curriculum, teachers and others must take into account those dance activities that can contribute to the needs of the individual and the group. Certain physiological and sociological principles based on a study of child growth and development readily point up some of the directions that might be taken when dance activities are selected to meet children's needs.

Teachers, supervisors, and others working together on a cooperative basis can help to identify more clearly the needs of children of a particular community. In this way they will not only contribute to the wise selection of dance curriculum content but will be in a position to make suitable placement of learning experiences at the various grade levels.

Interests of Children

Although needs and interests of children may be closely related, there are certain differences which should be taken into account when activities are selected for the dance curriculum. While interests are, for the most part, acquired as products of the environment, needs, particularly those of an individual nature, are more likely to be innate. Herein lies one of the main differences between the two criteria as far as the selection of dance activities is concerned. For example, a child may demonstrate a temporary interest in an activity that may not contribute to his needs at a certain age level. This interest may have perhaps been aroused because of the child's environment. In other words, an older brother or sister or parent might influence a child to develop an interest in an activity that might not contribute to his needs or which might even have a detrimental effect as far as his real needs are concerned.

In selecting dance activities, children's interests should be thoroughly explored. Sometimes when teachers are asked why a certain activity has not been included in the curriculum they may reply that the children are not interested in it and do not care to participate in it. This cannot be considered an entirely valid answer, because children should be given a fair opportunity to develop an interest in an activity. For example, some people feel that children at certain age levels are reluctant to accept an activity like creative dance. After this activity has been introduced, however, children almost always show sufficient interest and enthusiasm to justify inclusion of creative dance as a part of the program.

Perhaps the best source of needs and interests of children is their inherent physical, social, emotional, and intellectual traits and characteristics, and I will next turn to these.

DEVELOPMENTAL TRAITS AND CHARACTERISTICS OF CHILDREN

In discussing this particular topic I will first take into account some general traits and characteristics. This will be followed by a more specific delineation of traits and characteristics for each age level from 5 through 12.

General Traits and Characteristics of Children

During the range of age levels from 5 through 7, children begin their formal education. In our culture a child leaves the home for a part of the day to take his or her place in school with children of approximately the same chronological age. Not only are these children taking an important step toward becoming increasingly more independent and self-reliant, but as they learn they move from being highly self-centered individuals to becoming more socialized members of the group.

This age is ordinarily characterized by a certain lack of motor coordination, because the small muscles of the hands and fingers are not as well developed as the large muscles of the arms and legs. Thus, as children start their formal education, they need to use large crayons or pencils as one means of expressing themselves. The urge to action is expressed through movement, since the child lives in a world of movement, so to speak. Children at these age levels thrive on vigorous activity. They develop as they climb, run, jump, hop, skip, or keep time to music. An important physical factor at this age level is that the eyeball is increasing in size and the eyes muscles are developing. This is an important determinant in the child's readiness to see and read small print, and thus it involves a sequence from large print on charts to primer type in pre-primers and primers.

Even though children have a relatively short attention span, they are extremely curious about their environment. At this stage the teacher can capitalize upon the child's urge to learn by providing opportunities to gain information from first-hand experiences through the use of the senses. The child sees, hears, smells, feels, tastes, and *moves* in order to learn.

The age range from eight to ten is the period that usually marks the time spent in the third and fourth grades. Children now have a wider range of interests and a longer attention span. Although strongly individualistic, the child is working more from a position in a group. Games and dances should afford opportunities for developing and practicing skills in good leadership as well as in body control, strength, and endurance. Small muscles are developing, manipulative skills are increasing, and muscular coordination is improving. The eyes have developed to a point where many children can and do read more widely. The child is more capable of getting information from books and is beginning to learn more through vicarious experience. This is the stage in development when skills of communication (listening, speaking, reading, and writing) and the number system are needed to deal with situations both in and out of school.

Between the ages of 10 through 12 most children complete the fifth and sixth grades. This is a period of transition for most as they go from childhood into the pre-adolescent periods of their development. They may show concern over bodily changes and are sometimes self-conscious about appearance. At this stage children tend to differ widely in physical maturation and emotional stability. Greater deviations in development can be noticed within the sex groups than between them. Rate of physical growth can be rapid, sometimes showing itself in poor posture and restlessness. It is essential to recognize that prestige among peers is likely to be more important at this level than adult approval. During this period, the child is ready for a higher level of intellectual skills that involve reasoning, discerning fact from opinion, noting cause-and-effect relationships, drawing conclusions, and using various references to locate and compare validity of information. The child is beginning to show more proficiency in expression through oral and written communication.

Thus, from the years of kindergarten through completion of sixth grade, the child develops (1) *socially,* from a self-centered individual to a participating member of the group; (2) *emotionally,* from a state manifesting outbursts of anger to a higher degree of self-control; (3) *physically,* from childhood to the brink of adolescence; and (4) *intel-*

lectually, from learning by first-hand experiences to learning from technical and specialized resources.

If the child is to be educated as a growing organism, aspects of development need the utmost consideration in planning and guiding dance learning experiences that will be most profitable for the child at a particular stage of development.

Specific Traits and Characteristics of Children

The detailed description of the traits and characteristics given here includes the age levels 5 through 12. In examining the traits and characteristics, classroom teachers will no doubt profess greatest interest in those age levels which pertain most specifically to the grade level they are teaching or expect to teach. It is recommended, however, that consideration be given to the age levels that are on either side of the teacher's specific interest. In other words, it seems essential that the teacher have a full understanding of the children at the preceding grade level and a knowledge of the changes that will be inherent in traits and characteristics at the following grade level. Ideally, each classroom teacher should possess a general knowledge of the traits and characteristics of children at all age levels regardless of the specific grade level taught. The teacher is then in a better position to see the development of the child at a specific grade level as a part of his total growth and developmental patterns.

A special teacher responsible for teaching dance at all grade levels perhaps has little alternative but to develop a thorough understanding of the traits and characteristics of the entire age span of children 5–12. This knowledge seems essential if the special teacher is to do an adequate job of guiding, directing, and supervising dance learning experiences.

Traits and Characteristics of the Five-Year Old Child

Physical

2. Boys' height, 42 to 46 inches; weight, 38 to 49 pounds; girls' height, 42 to 46 inches; weight, 36 to 48 pounds.

2. May grow two or three inches and gain from three to six pounds during the year.
3. Girls may be about a year ahead of boys in physiological development.
4. Beginning to have better control of body.
5. The large muscles are better developed than the small muscles that control the fingers and hands.
6. Right or left handedness usually determined.
7. Eye and hand coordination is not complete.
8. May have farsighted vision.
9. Vigorous and noisy, but activity appears to have definite direction.
10. Tires easily and needs plenty of rest.
11. Can wash and take care of toilet needs.
12. Can use fork and spoon and may try to use knife.

Social

1. Interests in neighborhood games which involve any number of children.
2. Plays various games to test his skill.
3. Enjoys other children and likes to be with them.
4. Interests are largely self-centered.
5. Seems to get along best in small groups.
6. Shows an interest in home activities.
7. Imitates when he plays.
8. Gets along well in taking turns.
9. Respects the belongings of other people.

Emotional

1. Seldom shows jealousy toward younger siblings.
2. Usually sees only one way to do a thing.
3. Usually sees only one answer to a question.
4. Inclined not to change plans in the middle of an activity, but would rather begin over.

5. May fear being deprived of mother.
6. Some definite personality traits evidenced.
7. Is learning to get along better, but still may resort to quarreling and fighting.
8. Likes to be trusted with errands.
9. Enjoys performing simple tasks.
10. Wants to please and do what is expected of him.
11. Is beginning to sense right and wrong in terms of specific situations.

Intellectual

1. Enjoys copying designs, letters, and numbers.
2. Interested in completing tasks.
3. May tend to monopolize table conversation.
4. Frequently bothered by frightening dreams.
5. Memory for past events good.
6. Looks at books and pretends to read.
7. Likes recordings of words and music that tell a story.
8. Enjoys counting objects.
9. Over 2,000 words in vocabulary.
10. Can speak in complete sentences.
11. Can sing simple melodies, beat good rhythms, and recognize simple tunes.
12. Daydreams seem to center around make-believe play.
13. Attention span increasing up to 20 minutes in some cases.
14. Is able to plan activities.
15. Enjoys stories, dramatic play, and poems.
16. Enjoys making up dances to music.
17. Pronunciation is usually clear.
18. Can express his needs well in words.

Traits and Characteristics of the Six-Year Old Child

Physical

1. Boys' height, 44 to 48 inches; weight, 41 to 54 pounds; girls' height, 43 to 48 inches; weight, 40 to 53 pounds.

2. Growth is gradual in weight and height.
3. Milk teeth shedding and first permanent molars emerging.
4. Good appetite, and wants to eat between meals.
5. Good supply of energy.
6. Marked activity urge absorbs him in running, jumping, chasing, and dodging games.
7. Muscular control becoming more effective with large objects.
8. There is a noticeable change in the eye-hand behavior.
9. Legs lengthening rapidly.
10. Big muscles crave activity.

Social

1. Self-centered and has need for praise.
2. Likes to be first.
3. Indifferent to sex distinction.
4. Enjoys group play when groups tend to be small.
5. Likes parties but behavior may not always be decorous.
6. The majority enjoy school association and have a desire to learn.
7. Interested in conduct of friends.
8. Boys like to fight and wrestle with peers to prove masculinity.
9. Shows an interest in group approval.

Emotional

1. Restless and may have difficulty in making decisions.
2. Emotional patterns of anger may be difficult to control at times.
3. Behavior patterns may often be explosive and unpredictable.
4. Jealousy toward siblings at times; at other times takes pride in siblings.
5. Greatly excited by anything new.
6. Behavior becomes susceptible to shifts in direction, inwardly motivated and outwardly stimulated.
7. May be self-assertive and dramatic.

Intellectual

1. Vocabulary of over 2,500 words.
2. Interest span inclined to be short.
3. Knows number combinations adding up to ten.
4. Knows comparative values of the common coins.
5. Can define simple objects in terms of what they are used for.
6. Knows right and left side of body.
7. Has an association with creative activity and motorized life experience.
8. Drawings are crude but realistic and suggestive of early man.
9. Will contribute to guided group planning.
10. Conversation usually concerns his own experience and interests.
11. Curiosity is active and memory is strong.
12. Identifies himself with imaginary characters.

Traits and Characteristics of the Seven-Year Old Child

Physical

1. Boys' height, 46 to 51 inches; weight, 45 to 60 pounds; girls' height, 46 to 50 inches; weight, 44 to 59 pounds.
2. Big muscle activity predominates in interest and value.
3. More improvement in eye-hand coordination.
4. May grow two or three inches and gain three to five pounds in weight during the year.
5. Tires easily and shows fatigue in the afternoon.
6. Has slow reaction time.
7. Needs to sleep approximately eleven hours daily on average.
8. May have to be reminded at times about control of elimination.
9. Heart and lungs are smallest in proportion to body size.
10. General health may be precarious, with susceptibility to disease high and resistance low.
11. Endurance is relatively poor.
12. Coordination is improving, throwing and catching are becoming more accurate.
13. Whole-body movements are under better control.
14. Small accessory muscles developing.

15. Displays amazing amounts of vitality.

Social

1. Wants recognition for his individual achievements.
2. Sex differences are not of very great significance.
3. Not always a good loser.
4. Conversation often centers around family.
5. Learning to stand up for his own rights.
6. Interested in friends and is not influenced by their social or economic status.
7. May have nervous habits such as nail-biting, tongue-sucking, scratching or pulling at ear.
8. Attaining orientation in time.
9. Gets greater enjoyment from group play.
10. Shows greater signs of cooperative efforts.

Emotional

1. Curiosity and creative desires may condition responses.
2. May find it difficult to take criticism from adults.
3. Wants to be more independent.
4. Reaching for new experiences and trying to relate himself to enlarged world.
5. Overanxious to reach goals set by parents and teachers.
6. Critical of himself and sensitive to failure.
7. Emotional pattern of anger is more controlled.
8. Becoming less impulsive and boisterous in actions than at six.

Intellectual

1. Abstract thinking is barely beginning.
2. Is able to listen longer.
3. Reads some books by himself.
4. Is able to reason, but has little experience upon which to base judgments.

5. Attention span still short and retention poor; does not object to repetition.
6. Reaction time is still slow.
7. Learning to evaluate the achievements of self and others.
8. Concerned with own lack of skill and achievement.
9. Becoming more realistic and less imaginative.

Traits and Characteristics of the Eight-Year-Old Child

Physical

1. Boys' height, 48 to 53 inches; weight 49 to 70 pounds; girls' height, 48 to 52 inches; weight 47 to 66 pounds.
2. Interested in games requiring coordination of small muscles.
3. Arms are lengthening and hands are growing larger.
4. Eyes can accommodate more easily.
5. Some develop poor posture.
6. Accidents appear to occur more frequently at this age.
7. Fewer communicable diseases.
8. Appreciates correct skill performance.

Social

1. Girls are careful of their clothes but boys are not.
2. Leaves many things uncompleted.
3. Has special friends.
4. Has longer periods of peaceful play.
5. Does not like playing alone.
6. Enjoys dramatizing.
7. Starts collections.
8. Enjoys school and dislikes staying home.
9. Likes variety.
10. Recognition of property rights is well established.
11. Responds well to group activity.
12. Interest will focus on friends of own sex.
13. Beginning of the desire to become a member of the club.

Emotional

1. Dislikes taking much criticism from adults.
2. Can give and take criticism in his own group.
3. May develop enemies.
4. Does not like to be treated as a child.
5. Has a marked sense of humor.
6. First impulse is to blame others.
7. Becoming more realistic, wants to find out for himself.

Intellectual

1. Can tell day of month and year.
2. Voluntary attention span increasing.
3. Interested in far-off places; ways of communication now have real meaning.
4. Becoming more aware of adult world and his place in it.
5. Ready to tackle almost anything.
6. Shows a capacity for self-evaluation.
7. Like to memorize.
8. Not always good at telling time, but very much aware of it.

Traits and Characteristics of the Nine-Year-Old Child

Physical

1. Boys' height, 50 to 55 inches; weight, 55 to 74 pounds; girls' height, 50 to 54 inches; weight, 52 to 74 pounds.
2. Increasing strength in arms, hands, and fingers.
3. Endurance improving.
4. Needs and enjoys much activity; boys like to shout, wrestle, and tussle with each other.
5. A few girls near puberty.
6. Girls' growth maturity gaining over boys' up to two years.
7. Girls enjoy active group games but are usually less noisy and less full of spontaneous energy than boys.

8. Likely to slouch and assume unusual postures.
9. Eyes are much better developed and are able to accommodate to close work with less strain.
10. Needs ten to eleven hours sleep on the average; is a good sleeper, but often does not get enough sleep.
11. May tend to over-exercise.
12. Sex differences appear in recreational activities.
13. Interested in own body and wants to have questions answered.

Social

1. Wants to be like others, talk like others, and look like them.
2. Girls are becoming more interested in their clothes.
3. Is generally a conformist and may be afraid of that which is different.
4. Able to be on his own.
5. Able to be fairly responsible and dependable.
6. Some firm and loyal friendships may develop.
7. Increasing development of qualities of leadership.
8. Increasing interest in activities involving challenges and adventure.
9. Increasing participation in varied and organized group activities.

Emotional

1. May sometimes be outspoken and critical of the adults he knows, although he has a genuine fondness for them.
2. Responds best to adults who treat him as an individual and approach him in an adult way.
3. Likes recognition for what he has done and responds well to deserved praise.
4. Likely to be backward about public recognition, but likes private praise.
5. Developing sympathy and loyalty to others.
6. Does not mind criticism or punishment if he thinks it fair, but is indignant if he thinks it is unfair.

7. Disdainful of danger to and safety of himself, which may be a result of increasing interest in activities involving challenges and adventure.

Intellectual

1. Individual differences are clear and distinct.
2. Some real interests are beginning to develop.
3. Beginning to have a strong sense of right and wrong.
4. Understand explanations.
5. Interests are closer to those of ten- or eleven-year-olds than to those of seven- or eight-year-olds.
6. As soon as a project fails to hold interest, it may be dropped without further thought.
7. Attention span is greatly increased.
8. Seems to be guided best by a reason, simple and clear-cut, for a decision which needs to be made.
9. Ready to learn from occasional failure of his judgment as long as learning takes place in situations where failure will not have too serious consequences.
10. Able to make up own mind and come to decisions.
11. Marked reading disabilities begin to become more evident and may tend to influence the personality.
12. Discrepancy of interest in reading is becoming apparent: many are great readers while others may be barely interested in books.
13. Will average between six and seven words per remark.

Traits and Characteristics of the Ten-Year-Old Child

Physical

1. Boys' height, 52 to 57 inches; weight, 59 to 82 pounds; girls' height, 52 to 57 inches; weight 57 to 83 pounds.
2. Stability in growth rate and stability of physiological processes.
3. Physically active and likes to rush around and be busy.
4. Before the onset of puberty there is usually a resting period or

plateau, during which the boy or girl does not appear to gain in either height or weight.
5. Interested in the development of more skills.
6. Reaction time is improving.
7. Muscular strength does not seem to keep pace with growth.
8. Refining and elaborating skill in the use of small muscles.

Social

1. Begins to recognize the fallibility of adults.
2. Moving more onto a peer-centered society.
3. Both boys and girls are amazingly self-dependent.
4. Self-reliance has grown, and at the same time intensified group feelings are required.
5. Divergence between the two sexes is widening.
6. Great team loyalties are developing.
7. Beginning to identify with one's social contemporaries of the same sex.
8. Individuality is well defined and insights are more mature.
9. Accepts appeals to reason with relative ease.
10. On the whole he has a fairly critical sense of justice.
11. Boys show their friendship with other boys by wrestling and jostling with each other, while girls walk around with arms around each other as friends.
12. Interest in people, in the community and in affairs of the world is keen.
13. Interested in social problems in an elementary way; likes to take part in discussions.

Emotional

1. Increasing tendency to rebel against adult domination.
2. Capable of loyalties and hero worship, and can inspire it in his schoolmates.
3. Can be readily inspired to group loyalties in his club organization.

4. Likes the sense of solidarity which comes from keeping a group secret as a member of a group.
5. Girls dramatize with paper dolls many life situations in whispered secrets or in outspoken dialogue.
6. Each sex has an increasing tendency to show lack of sympathy and understanding for the other.
7. Boys' and girls' behavior and interests becoming increasingly different.

Intellectual

1. Works with executive speed and likes the challenge of mathematics.
2. Shows a capacity to budget time and energy.
3. Can attend to a visual task and at the same time maintain conversation.
4. Some become discouraged and may give up trying when unsuccessful.
5. The attention span has lengthened considerably, with the child able to listen to and follow directions and retain knowledge more easily.
6. Beginning to understand real causal relations.
7. Making finer conceptual distinctions and thinking reflectively.
8. Developing scientific approach.
9. Better oriented with respect to time.
10. Ready to plan the day and accept responsibility for getting things done on time.

Traits and Characteristics of the Eleven-Year-Old Child

Physical

1. Boys' height, 53 to 58 inches; weight, 64 to 91 pounds; girls' height, 53 to 59 inches; weight, 64 to 95 pounds.
2. Marked changes in muscle system causing awkwardness and habits sometimes distressing to the child.

3. Shows fatigue more easily.
4. Some girls and a few boys suddenly show rapid growth and evidence of the approach of adolescence.
5. In general this is a period of good health with fewer diseases and infections.
6. On the average girls may be taller and heavier than boys.
7. Uneven growth of different parts of the body.
8. Rapid growth may result in laziness in the lateral type of child, and fatigue and irritability in the linear type.
9. Willing to work hard at acquiring physical skills, and puts emphasis on excellence of performance of physical feats.
10. Boys are more active and rough in games than girls.
11. Eye-hand coordination well developed.
12. Body growth is more rapid than heart growth, and lungs are not fully developed.
13. Boys develop greater power in shoulder girdle muscles.

Social

1. Internal guiding standards have been set up and, although guided by what other children do, he will modify his behavior in line with those internal standards.
2. Does a number of things because they are socially acceptable rather than out of a sense of right and wrong.
3. Although obsessed by standards of peers, he is anxious for social approval from adults.
4. Need for social life companionship of children of own age.
5. Liking for organized games more and more prominent.
6. Girls are likely to be self-conscious in the presence of boys and are usually much more mature than boys.
7. Team spirit is very strong.
8. Boys' and girls' interests are not always the same, and there may be some antagonism between the sexes.
9. Often engages in silly behavior, such as giggling and clowning.
10. Girls are more interested in social appearance than boys.

Emotional

1. If unskilled in group games and game skills, he may tend to withdraw.
2. Boys may be concerned if they feel they are underdeveloped.
3. Moods change quickly.
4. May appear to be indifferent and uncooperative.
5. Wants to grow up, but may be afraid to leave childhood security behind.
6. Increase in self-direction and in a serious attitude toward work.
7. Need for approval to feel secure.
8. Beginning to have a fully developed idea of own importance.

Intellectual

1. Increasing power of attention and abstract reasoning.
2. Able to maintain a longer period of intellectual activity between first hand experiences.
3. Interested in scientific experiments and procedures.
4. Can carry out many individual intellectual responsibilities.
5. Able to discuss problems and to see different sides of questions.
6. May lack maturity of judgment.
7. Increased language facility.
8. Attention span is increasing and concentration may be given to a task for a long period of time.
9. Level of aspiration is increased.
10. Growing ability to use several facts to make a decision.
11. Insight into causal relationships is developing more and is manifested by many "why" and "how" questions.

Traits and Characteristics of the Twelve-Year-Old Child

Physical

1. Boys' height, 55 to 61 inches; weight, 70 to 101 pounds; girls' height, 56 to 62 inches; weight, 71 to 107 pounds.
2. Becoming more skillful in the use of small muscles.
3. May be relatively little body change in some cases.

4. Ten hours of sleep is considered average.
5. Heart rate at rest is between 80 and 90.

Social

1. Increasing identification of self with other children of his own sex.
2. Increasing recognition of fallibility of adults.
3. May see himself as a child and adults as adults.
4. Getting ready to make the difficult transition to adolescence.
5. Pressure is being placed on individual at this level to begin to assume adult responsibilities.

Emotional

1. Beginning to develop a truer picture of morality.
2. Clearer understanding of real causal relations.
3. The process of sexual maturation involves structural and physiological changes with possible perplexiing and disturbing emotional problems.
4. Personal appearance may become a source of great conflict and learning to appreciate good grooming or the reverse may be prevalent.
5. May be very easily hurt when criticized or made the scapegoat.
6. Maladjustments may occur when there is not a harmonious relationship between child and adult.

Intellectual

1. Learns more ways of studying and controlling the physical world.
2. The use of language (on many occasions his own vocabulary) to exchange ideas or for purposes of explanation.
3. More use of reflective thinking and greater ease of distinction.
4. Continuation in development of scientific approach.

These lists of traits and characteristics from 5 to 12 years of age were assembled through a documentary analysis of a large number of sources that have appeared in the literature over the years. It should be understood that these traits and characteristics are suggestive of the behavior patterns of the so-called normal child. If a child does not conform to all these traits and characteristics, this should not be interpreted to mean that he or she is seriously deviating from the normal. Each child progresses at his or her own rate, and there will be much overlapping of the traits and characteristics listed for each age level. A case in point are the ranges of heights and weights. These heights and weights are what might be called a range within a range, and are computed means or averages within larger ranges. In other words, children at a given age level could possibly weigh much more or less and be much taller or shorter than the ranges indicate. To illustrate how wide a range can be, one study of large numbers of children showed that eleven-year-old girls ranged in weight from 45 to 180 pounds.

As an interesting experiment the reader might wish to examine the 300 traits and characteristics and sort out some of them for the purpose of comparing them with the degree of difficulty and complexity of various dance forms. This will give some idea of one average child's capacity for and interest in performing these activities.

CHAPTER 6

BASIC DANCE MOVEMENTS

One of the most important characteristics of life is movement. Whatever else they may involve, all of man's achievements are based upon his ability to move. Obviously, the very young child is not endowed with intelligence in the sense of abstract thought, and he only gradually acquires the ability to deal with symbols and intellectualize his experience in the course of development. On the other hand, the child is a creature of movement and feeling. Any effort to educate the child must take this dominance of movement in the life of the child into account.

For the young child, being able to move as effectively and efficiently as possible is directly related to the proficiency with which he is able to perform the various fundamental motor skills. In turn, the success he will have in dance activities which require certain motor skills will depend on his proficiency in performing these skills. Thus, effective and efficient movement is prerequisite to the performance of basic motor skills needs for success in most dance activities.

Motor skill is judged according to the degree of proficiency with which a given bodily movement is performed. This is to say that a skill is a scientific way of moving the body and/or its segments so as to expend a minimum amount of energy while achieving maxiumum results. Years ago neurophysiologists suggested that all skills consist in the putting together of simple natural movements, of which we have only about 200, in unusual or complex combinations in order to achieve a given objective. The best mode of performing specific skills has been arrived at by scientific insight from such fields as anatomy and kinesiology, which suggest how the body can move to achieve maximum efficiency.

Other things being equal, the individual's degree of profiency in the performance of a skill is directly related to his or her innate capacity; that is, each individual is endowed with a certain amount of native ability. Through such factors as good teaching, motivation, and the like, attempts are made to help children perform to the best of their particular ability and attain the highest level of skill.

Basic dance movements, considered as basic motor skills, can be placed into the two broad categories of *locomotor* movements and *axial* movements.

LOCOMOTOR MOVEMENTS

Locomotor movements involve changes in body position that propel the body over the surface area, with the impetus being given by the feet and legs. There are five basic types: walking, running, leaping, jumping, and hopping, and three combination movements: galloping, skipping, and sliding. The first five of these are performed with an even rhythm and the last three with an uneven rhythm. Locomotor movements require a certain amount of strength and the development of important sensory-motor mechanisms concerned with balance. They also require various degrees of neuromotor coordination for proficient performance.

All of the locomotor movements should be learned correctly by the elementary school-age child. The reason is that these movements comprise the basic requirements for proficiency of performance in the activities contained in a well-planned dance program for children. Teachers should have certain basic knowledge about the locomotor movements so that they will be alert to improve performance of them. The following generalized information is intended for this purpose.

Walking

Walking is the child's first experience with bipedal locomotion. He starts to propel himself over the surface area with uneven, full-sole steps (flatfootedness). At this time he is generally referred to as a "toddler," a term perhaps derived from the word "tottering." He appears to be tottering to keep in an upright position, which is indicative of the problems he is having with balance and the force of gravity. At about four years of age, on the average, the child's pattern of walking approximates that of an adult.

Ordinarily, when the child is learning to walk, his only teachers are his family members. Because of this, he is not likely to benefit from instruction on correct procedure, and the very important aspect of foot position may thus be overlooked. It is possibly for this reason that many children enter school walking in various degrees of the "toeing out" position rather than pointing the toes straight ahead. Poor walking habits, if allowed to persist, can place undue strain on certain body parts that in turn impede proficiency of body movement.

Walking involves transferring the weight from one foot to the other. The walk is started with a push-off backwards against the surface area with the ball and toes of the foot. After this initial movement the leg swings forward from the hip, the heel of the other foot is set down, the outer half of the foot next, and then the next push-off is made with toes pointing straight ahead. Educationally, walking is used in such activities as walking to rhythmical accompaniment, combining the walk with other movements in various dance activities, walking about in movement songs, and walking around a circle in certain circle dances.

Running

At about 18 months of age the average child develops a movement that appears to be something between a walk and a run: the walking pattern is accelerated, but does not approximate running form. It is usually not before ages five or six that the child's running form becomes similar to that used by an adult. As the child gets older he is able to increase his speed of running as well as his ability to run greater distances.

Like walking, running involves transferring the weight from one foot to the other, but the rate of speed is increased. The ball of the foot touches the surface area first, and the toes point straight ahead. The body is suspended in the air for a moment in which there is no contact with the surface area. This differs from the walk, in which contact of one or the other foot with the surface area is always maintained. In the run there is more flexion at the knee, which involves a higher leg lift. There is also a higher arm lift, with flexion at the elbow reaching more or less a right angle. In running, there is more of a forward body lean than in walking, and in both cases the head points straight ahead. In many instances the child who has not been taught to run correctly will violate certain mechanical principles by having a backward rather than a forward lean, carrying the arms too high, and turning the head to the side rather than looking straight ahead.

Running is used in dance activities where there is a quickened pace from the walk. It is also used in combination with other locomotor movements, particularly in some creative dance themes.

Leaping

Leaping may be one of the most misunderstood of the locomotor movements. Sports announcers erroneously refer to some athletes as "leapers" when they should be saying "jumpers." And, often cynical critics of modern dance refer to it as "jumping across the stage."

Leaping, like walking and running, is performed with an even rhythm like a slow run, with one essential difference: the push-off is up and then forward, with the feeling of suspension "up and over." The landing should be on the ball of the foot with sufficient flexion at the knee to absorb the shock.

Leaping is not used as a specific locomotor movement in very many dance activities. One exception is its use in certain creative dance forms.

Jumping

In a sense, jumping is somewhat similar to walking and running in its movement pattern. However, jumping requires elevation of the body off the surface area, and thus more strength is needed to apply force for this purpose. Usually, the child's first experience with a movement approximating jumping occurs when he steps from a higher to a lower level, as in the case of going downstairs. Although there are many variations in the jumping performance of children, generally speaking they tend to improve as they get older, with improvement tending to be more pronounced for boys than for girls.

Jumping is accomplished by pushing off with both feet and landing on both feet or pushing off with one foot and landing on both feet. Since absorption of shock is important in jumping, the landing should occur with flexed knees and on the balls of the feet.

The jump may be used by children in certain aspects of creative dance. Some structured dances require the jump as a basic movement. A case in point is the Scandinavian folk dance, *Seven Jumps.*

Hopping

While hopping may be the least difficult of the "even" locomotor movements to describe, it may be the most difficult to execute. Hopping involves taking off and landing on the same foot. Thus, hopping is more complex than the jump, because the body is elevated from the surface area by the action of only one foot. Not only is greater strength needed for the hop, but also a more refined adjustment of balance owing to the smaller base of support.

Hopping is used as a specific step in some dance activities. For example, in such a dance step as the *schottische* the pattern is step-step-step-hop-step-hop-step-hop.

Even though hopping is a skill not used in many dance activities, one of the more important reasons why children should become proficient in this locomotor movement is that it can help them regain balance in any kind of situation where they have temporarily "lost their footing." When this occurs, the child can use the hop to keep his balance and remain in an upright position while getting the temporarily incapacitated foot into action.

Galloping

The locomotor movement of galloping is a combination of the basic patterns of walking and leaping and is performed with an uneven rhythm. Since an uneven rhythmic movement requires more neuromotor coordination, the ability to gallop is developed later than those locomotor movements requiring an even rhythm. The child is likely to learn to gallop before he learns to skip and about one-half of the children are able to perform at least an approximation of a galloping movement by about the age of four. Between the ages of six and seven most children can perform this movement.

Galloping can be explained by pretending that one foot is injured. A step is taken with the lead foot, but the "injured" foot can bear little weight and is brought up only behind the other foot and not beyond it. A transfer of weight is made to the lead foot, and thus a gallop is really a fast limp.

One of the most important factors about learning to gallop is that it helps children learn to change direction in a forward and backward plane more easily. Backward galloping can be done by starting with the lead foot to the back. If a child is proficient in galloping he will likely be more successful in dance activities that require a forward and/or backward movement.

Galloping as a basic dance movement in combination with the skip is used in the forward *polka*. It also has an important use as a fundamental movement when children become "galloping horses" to appropriate rhythmical accompaniment.

Skipping

Although skipping requires more coordination than galloping, some children will perform variations of the skip around four years of age. With proper instruction, a majority of children should be able to accomplish this movement by age six.

Skipping can be taught from the walk. A strong push-off should be emphasized. The push-off should be such a forceful upward one that the foot leaves the surface area. In order to maintain balance a hop is taken. The sequence is step, push-off high, hop. The hop occurs on the same foot that was pushing off, and this is the skip. The difference of the two actions is what gives the skip its uneven rhythm, with a strong or long action (step) and a short one (hop).

Skipping finds use as a fundamental locomotor movement when children skip to musical accompaniment, when used in certain movement songs, and when skipping around in a circle in certain circle dances. It can also be combined with other locomotor movements, as in the case of the aforementioned forward polka.

Sliding

Sliding is much the same as the gallop, but movement is in a sideward direction or lateral plane. One foot is drawn up to the lead foot; weight is shifted from the lead foot to the drawing foot and back again.

An important feature of gaining proficiency in sliding is that it helps the child to be able to change direction skillfully in a lateral plane. When a child has developed the skill of sliding from side to side, he does not have to cross his feet and thus can change directions more easily in dances requiring this movement. Sliding is used in certain circle dances when it replaces the walk or skip. It is also used in certain partner dances in what used to be identified as social dancing.

Combining Locomotor Movements

A few examples of combination locomotor movements have already been given, and there are numerous other possibilities. An excellent source of combinations of basic locomotor movements is found in the recommendations of the National Dance Association Task Force on Children's Dance. Some of these recommendations follow:

1. Phrases of each one of these movements for children should be

long, the change from one to the other possibly being made on a signal from the teacher.

2. Later, a specific number of pulse beats can be given in equal phrase lengths, such as 8 and 8, accompanied by two different pulse beat sounds, as the following: clap 8 and count 8; use two different notes on the piano; use the head and side of a drum.

3. Still later, children can try short and/or uneven phrase lengths and make their own combinations, changing on different but rhythmically related count sequences.

In the following combinations, the run has not been used so that the pulse interval for the different movements may be identical. When accompaniment is used, a sequence of quarter notes or of moderate beats with equal intervals in sufficient. The monotony of the sound can be relieved, however, by breaking up the pulse beat with occasional patterns, or playing only accents at times.

Movement Combination	Example	Description
Walk and Jump	WWWWWW JJJJ	Alternate feet with weight change; then with two feet, no weight change
Jump and Hop	JJJJHHHH	Two feet, no weight change; then with one foot; no weight change
Walk and Hop	WWWHHH	Alternate feet with weight change; then with one foot, no weight change[1]

In my own experience I have found it useful to acquaint children with *cadence* in order to improve upon rhythm. Theoretically, this refers to the number of steps or paces taken over a period of time or

[1] American Alliance for Health, Physical Education, Recreation and Dance, *Children's Dance*, rev. ed., (Washington, D.C., 1981), p. 16.

accompaniment tempo. If one were to have children perform the fundamental locomotor movement of walking to the accompaniment, this could be done at the tempo of four beats to the *measure* in 4-4 time. This is shown in the following score with *quarter* notes. The quarter note is referred to as a *walk* note.

♩ ♩ ♩ ♩

Accompaniment for running is twice as fast and is depicted with *eighth* notes (*run* notes as in the following score).

♪ ♪ ♪ ♪ ♪ ♪ ♪ ♪

Many different sequences of walking and running can be used by various beats as follows:

walk, walk, run   ♩ ♩ ♪

walk, walk, run, run, run   ♩ ♩ ♪ ♪ ♪

run, run, walk, run, run, walk   ♪ ♪ ♩ ♪ ♪ ♩

walk, walk, run, run, run, run   ♩ ♩ ♪ ♪ ♪ ♪

A walk and run note can be used together for the uneven locomotor movements of skipping, galloping, and sliding. The following example depicts the use of this for skipping (step-hop).

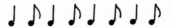

♩ ♪ ♩ ♪ ♩ ♪ ♩ ♪

In addition to drum accompaniment suggested above and controlled by the teacher, many records provide musical accompaniment for the performance of the various locomotor movements (see in particular record sources 7, 10, 14, 19).

The information presented here is merely suggestive, and the creative teacher, with the collaboration of the children, can develop many exciting aspects of locomotor movement combinations. As will be seen in Chapter 8 any manner of forms of locomotion and combinations thereof can be used in the simple and more complex structured dances.

Teaching Locomotor Movements

There are at least two approaches to the teaching of locomotor movements to primary level children. One concerns teaching them as separate entities or more or less in isolation from activities in which the movements are inherent. The second involves teaching the movements as a part of a given activity. Each of these will be taken into account in the following discussions.

The following procedures are submitted as suggestive points of departure that the teacher may take in providing locomotor learning experiences for children by teaching them the specific movements.

1. Play accompaniment so that children can listen to it.
2. Have the children describe the accompaniment in terms of what it sounded like to them.
3. Ask what they might do to the accompaniment in terms of what it sounded like to them.
3. Ask what they might do to the accompaniment, such as walk, run, skip, etc.
4. Let them clap to get the tempo of the accompaniment.
5. Let them try the locomotor movement.
6. Select some children or volunteers, play the accompaniment again, and have the other children observe them.
7. Have the children evaluate good features of the performers. ("What did you like about the way they did it?")
8. Have all the children do the activity again, analyzing their own performance.

(In connection with the above procedure it is suggested that the reader review the section on "Phases of the Teaching-Learning Situation" in Chapter 3).

As indicated previously, the second approach is concerned with teaching locomotor movements through the children's participation in an activity in which the movements are inherent. I have found it valuable to prepare stories to be read to the children for this purpose. Following is one of my own prepared stories containing the locomotor movements of walking and running.

LITTLE RED EAGLE'S DRUM

Little Red Eagle is an Indian Boy.
He lives in an Indian village with his father and mother.
One day Little Red Eagle's father gave him a drum.
Little Red Eagle likes to hit his drum with his hand.
He can make his drum talk.
He makes it talk by hitting it with his hand.
Sometimes the drum goes fast.
It says, "Run, run, run."
Sometimes it goes slow.
It says, "Walk, walk, walk."
Other times it goes fast and slow.
Then it says, "Run, run, run, walk, walk, walk."
The Little Indian boys and girls hear Red Eagle's drum.
Soon they can do what the drum tells them.
When the drum goes fast, they run.
When the drum goes slow, they walk.
When the drum goes fast and slow, they run and then walk.
When the drum stops talking, the boys and girls stop.
The children like to hear Little Red Eagle's talking drum.
Let us see if we can make the drum tell us what to do.

The following simulated teaching–learning situation suggests how this approach might be used.

TEACHER: Boys and girls, remember the other day when we sang the song "Ten Little Indians?"

(CHILDREN)

TEACHER: Today I would like to read a story about some little Indian boys and girls. (Teacher reads the story and with various degrees of guidance the children engage in the activity. The teacher is alert to observe performance and to assist children as needed. Some children are selcted to provide the drum accompaniment. After a time the activity is stopped and the teacher evaluates it with the children).

TEACHER: What were some of the things you liked about acting out the story?

(CHILDREN)

TEACHER: Yes, some children bumped into each other. What could be do about that?

(CHILDREN)

TEACHER: I noticed that all of you kept getting better and better as you listened to the drum to tell what to do. Let's try it again sometime. Maybe we could do skipping and galloping as well as walking and running.

These two approaches are somewhat analogous to the teaching of reading. Some reading specialists believe that at the early age levels "sight reading" should be the predominant practice. Others hold to the notion that children should start with phonics (aspects of reading skills). What should be understood, whether for teaching reading or locomotor movements, is that all children do not necessarily learn in the same way. Therefore, rather than using either approach in absolute form, a combination of the two might well be considered.

AXIAL MOVEMENTS

Axial movements are nonlocomotor in nature. They can be performed either with some parts of the body remaining in contact with the surface area or with the body as a whole in gross movement. Included among the axial movements are swinging, bending, stretching, pulling, pushing, and the rotation movements of turning and twisting. In fact, it has been suggested that nonlocomotor movements that are identifiable through their names as specific ways of moving are legion. Such action words as push, pull, strike, dodge, lift, freeze, kick, spin, shake, sway, reach, collapse, turn and similar verbs are all combinations of basic locomotor movements. Teachers can make their own lists of such action words and use them as catalysts for exploration and improvisation.[2]

Many of the axial movements are required at one time or another in the performance of various dance activities. Proficiency in the performance of the axial movements will improve this performance of locomotor movements; for example, the importance of arm swinging in running. When children can perform the axial movements with grace and facility there is a minimum expenditure of energy, and better performance results.

AUXILIARY MOVEMENTS

There are certain movements that may not ordinarily be classified as either locomotor or axial. However, they are very important in the successful performance of some dance activities. These movements are identified here as auxiliary movements, since they are auxiliary to the cessation of movement. Among some of the more important as far as dance activities are concerned are those directly associated with *stopping, falling,* and *landing.*

Stopping

It may sound ludicrous to emphasize the important of stopping, especially because structured dances stop on a beat with little risk of any loss of balance. Oftentimes, however, certain creative dance themes may require a quick and sudden stop. Therefore, children should be given an opportunity to develop the ability to do this.

Two ways of stopping are the *stride* stop and the *skip* stop. The

[2] *Ibid.,* p. 17.

stride stop involves stopping in running stride. There is flexion at the knees and a slight backward lean to maintain balance. This method of stopping can be used when the performer is moving at slow speed. The skip stop should be used when there is fast movement and the performer needs to come to a quick stop. This is accomplished with a hop on either foot, the other foot making contact with the surface area almost simultaneously. Because of the latter movement, this method of stopping is sometimes called the *jump* stop, as the performer appears to be landing on both feet at the same time.

Stopping can be practiced in an activity situation called *Start and Stop*. In this activity the children are in a straight line some distance away. The teacher calls, "Start," and on this signal all children run forward as the teacher sounds run notes on a drum. When the drum beat ceases, anyone moving must return to the starting line. This procedure is continued until one or more children have reached the goal line. The teacher should be alert to detect good stopping form.

Falling

In those activities that require saying in an upright position, emphasis, of course, should be on maintaining this position. Nevertheless, there are occasions when a performer loses balance and falls to the surface area. Whenever possible, a fall should be taken in such a way that injury is least likely to occur. One way to accomplish this is to attempt to "break the fall" with the hands. Relaxation and flexion at the joints that put the performer in a "bunched" position are helpful in avoiding injury when falling to the surface area.

Landing

Landing is concerned with the body coming to the surface area from a height or distance. Absorption when landing is accomplished by bending the knees. The weight is on the balls of the feet, and there is flexion at the ankle and knee joints. After landing the performer comes to an upright position with the arms in a sideward position so as to keep the body in balance.

There are some creative dance themes where children may execute a jump from the surface area. Without proper instruction some children tend to land in a "stiff kneed" position, thus exposing themselves to possible injury.

A concern among adult performers—and in some cases children as well—is the danger of dance injuries. Perhaps some of these injuries might be avoided if dancers would start at an early age to develop the auxiliary movements as a skill.

CHAPTER 7

CREATIVE DANCE

The word "creative" derives from the Latin word *creatus*, one meaning of which is "produced through imaginative skill." This meaning is compatible with one of the principles of learning as applied to dance that I cited in Chapter 3; that is, "The child should be given sufficient freedom to create his own responses in the situation he faces."

In Chapter 1 I reported that there may be a slight trend to include more in the way of creative dance for children in the modern elementary school. This trend appears to be slight indeed, and as far as the broad area of dance activities is concerned there has been a widespread neglect of creative dance for children over the years.

This is borne out by the various surveys that I have made, which invariably indicate that creative dance experiences for children are provided on a minimal basis.

It is not only unfortunate, but paradoxical, that more widespread use of creative dance has not prevailed, given the importance of creativity in the life of the child. Creative experience involves *self*-expression. It is concerned with the need to experiment, to express original ideas, to think, to react. Creativity and childhood enjoy a congruous relationship in that children are naturally creative. They imagine. They pretend. They are uninhibited. They are not only original but actually ingenious in their thoughts and actions. Indeed, creativity is a characteristic inherent in the lives of practically all children, although in various degrees. Some children create as a natural form of expression without adult stimulation, others may need a certain amount of teacher guidance and encouragement.

Such art forms as drawing, music, and writing are traditionally regarded as the best approaches to creative expression. The very essence of creative expression, however, is *movement*. Movement as a form of creativity utilizes the body as the instrument of expression, and especially for the young child this is the most natural form of creative expression. Because of their nature, children have an inclination to movement. It is the child's universal language, a most important form of communication and a most meaningful way of learning.

One of the greatest concerns to educators in a modern democratic society is the problem of how to provide for creative expression so that a child may develop his potentialities to the fullest. Democracy is only beginning to understand the power of the individual as perhaps the most dynamic force in the world today. It is in this frame of reference that the importance of creativity should become clear, because many of the problems in our complex society can be solved only through creative thinking. It has been my personal experience that creative dance for children, if properly conceived and conducted, can help to reach this objective.

ELEMENTS OF MOVEMENT

All aspects of movement involve certain important elements. These include *time, force,* and *space,* all of which are highly interrelated in the execution of any bodily movement. An authoritative description of the relationship of these elements is provided by Gladys Andrews Fleming:[1] Movement cannot be considered in isolation from the related elements of space, time, and force. As we begin to work with young children in the area of dance, we soon realize how these ele-

[1] Gladys Andrews, Fleming, *Creative Rhythmic Movement, Boys and Girls Dancing,* 2nd ed., Englewood Cliffs, 1976), p. 48.

ments are related to one another, as well as to movement as a whole. In working on the basic movement of *walk*, for example, these elements are "felt" and observable. When children move or walk in an area, they become aware of space by moving *through* space, by going in a certain *direction*, by traveling in a "high" or "low" *level* in space, and by using specific *amounts* of space. As they progress with their walk, *timing* is involved. They are moving in space at a certain *rate* of speed or with varying speeds, using time in their movement. Often they may respond to a specific pulse, which is simply a way of saying that their time is organized. In addition a third element, that of *force*, must be considered. Force both initiates the walking movement and determines its "quality;" amount of strength or intensity of the energy used can make a strong, hard walk of a soft, easy flowing walk.

Although these elements are mutually interdependent and interrelated, each of them still needs to be considered as a separate entity if one is to fully understand the part each plays in the whole movement. The following discussions of time, force, and space as they relate to creative movement should be viewed within this general frame of reference.

Time

Perhaps the two most important aspects of time in movement are *duration* and *tempo*. Duration is concerned with how long it takes to complete a movement. For example, a movement can be slow and deliberate, such as when a child attempts to create a movement to depict a falling snowflake. On the other hand, a movement might be made with sudden quickness, as in a dance activity involving a quick turn and stop.

Tempo is the rate of a regular pulse which measures the time within which the movements are performed. This is seen, for example, in the previous comment regarding the measured pulse (meter) of walk and run notes, with the run being twice as fast as the walk (the walk note being a quarter note and the run note being an eighth note).

Thus, duration measures the motion from start to finish; tempo measures the time within which all the motions take place. A movement of long duration, therefore, can take place within a fast tempo, and a movement of short duration can occur within a slow tempo.

Teachers can help children with the concept of tempo in movement with such questions as: Does the drum say fast or slow? How fast? How slow?

Force

Force needs to be applied in order to set the body or one of its segments in motion, and to change its speed and/or direction. Thus, force is concerned with the strength required for a given movement. Swinging the arms requires less strength than attempting to propel the body over the surface area with a graceful leap.

Geraldine Dimondstein,[2] a notable writer on the subject, once put the concept of force and movement into fine perspective: As a concept, movement is affected by force in the following ways: (1) by the external forces of gravity and momentum, (2) by the control and flow of energy applied to the muscles, and (3) by the speed of a movement against a resistant force (real or imagined).

As an expressive element, force as tension is created by degrees of resistance in the body, and is sensed kinesthetically as *muscle tension.* A child can increase the feeling or awareness of tension in many ways. Most basic perhaps are those which heighten an awareness of his own center of gravity and his sense of balance with the transference of body weight. Although the center of gravity refers to the point from which energy is released or controlled, there is no specific "point" located in the same place on every child. It is actually the vertical, horizontal, and lateral planes which intersect somewhere within the center of the torso.

A child may, however, locate his center or "middle" when he places his feet together and is standing erect. At the same time, he can sense that as soon as he moves from an aligned position, either by moving any part of his body in space or by taking a step, there is a change in the distribution of body weight. Through experimenting with dif-

[2] Geraldine Dimondstein, *Children Dance in the Classroom,* (New York: Macmillan), 1971, pp. 175–176.

ferent parts of movement he soon realizes that *body weight* and *balance* are closely related.

Force, as an essential element of dance, is experienced as the amount of tension or stress of movement. It may be defined as the flow and control of energy. Children experience qualities of force as greater or lesser tension, resistance or acquiescence to the pull of gravity, heaviness, or lightness. By varying the amount of energy in alternate ways, children become aware of different qualities of movement.

Space

Space is concerned with several important aspects of movement, among which are *direction, levels, range,* and *focus*. Direction simply means where one is going in space—forward, backward, sideways. Levels in space concern the level at which a child moves—high, middle, low. Range refers to the amount of space used and also to shapes made in space. Ordinarily the extremes of shapes are "large" and "small." Focus means "fixing" on a given point and moving in that direction.

In creative dance two very important factors are the amount of space required to perform a particular movement and the utilization of available space. With regard to the latter, it has been suggested that young children, during non-structured, self-initiated dance activities, seem to reveal differences in the quantity of space they use, and that these differences may be associated in important ways with other aspects of the child's development. Some studies tend to support the concept that space utilization of the young child in active play is a relatively stable dimension of his patterned behavior.

The above elements enter into all bodily movements in various degrees. The degree to which each is used effectively in combination will determine the extent to which a given movement is performed with skill, and thus the contribution to the enjoyment a child will derive from his or her creative dance experiences.

CLASSIFICATION OF CREATIVE DANCE

It is an arbitrary matter whether or not one makes an attempt to classify creative dance. However, I have found it useful to do so, especially when dealing with inexperienced teachers, because of the wide range of possibilities offered by creative dance. Therefore, the two classifications suggested here are designated as *individual interpretation* and *dramatization*. The essential difference between the two is in the degree of structuring of the activities.

Individual Interpretation

Individual interpretation has little structuring and in its extreme form involves children moving the way the accompaniment makes them feel; that is, the ideas for movement are supposed to originate with the children. This is perhaps analogous to what Mary Joyce[3] has termed "free dancing," in which everyone dances at the same time to whatever music is played. She recommends introducing free dancing as a challenge about halfway through a semester, using such a question as "Do you think you could dance to whatever music I put on?" She makes additional recommendations as follows. Play some movie background music, some dramatic orchestral music, some rhythmic folk music, and perhaps something classical or popular. Tell the children they must begin to move the minute they hear a sound and when the sound stops they are to hold their shapes and wait for the next selection. No time should be spent thinking or planning; a free dance must be a physical response to the music. Ask them to imagine that the music is coming from inside them and making their bodies move through space. Play a selection for only a few seconds. Then turn the volume off. Choose selections that differ decidedly in style, texture, and speed. The children find the surprise exciting. Often they bring in their own records. No one watches a free dance, not even the teacher. This dance should be improvisational and purely for personal satisfaction. Evaluation of each child's development, as-

---

[3] Mary, Joyce, *First Steps in Teaching Creative Dance to Children*, 2d ed., (Palo Alto, Cal., 1980), p. 44.

similation of the elements, ability to find variations, make choices, and solve movement problems can be done during the main part of the session as the teacher watches the whole class, half the class, or groups. Free dancing should remain completely free, by and for the child personally.

As I have mentioned previously, in individual interpretation, ideas for movement originate with the children. Although some children might be influenced by others, the movement that each child makes to the accompaniment is likely to be unique, different from other members of the group.

Individual interpretation might be perceived in the following manner: The accompaniment is received through the auditory sense. It is "syphoned" through the human organism and nervous system and the child reacts with a movement which expresses the way the accompaniment makes him feel.

One of the important aspects of individual interpretation lies in the selection of the proper kind of accompaniment. This is to say that accompaniment should be sensitive enough to depict different kinds of moods for the physical expression of one's feelings. (A particularly good source of accompaniment that I have found for individual interpretation is Album No. 4, parts V and VI of No. 11 on the record sources.)

Dramatization

Dramatization centers around some sort of story, plan, or idea which can provide various kinds of clues for children. It can involve (1) a story or idea that the children already know about or something with which they are familiar, (2) a story made up by the teacher, or (3) a story started by the teacher and added to by the children.

In using a familiar story such as "Jack and the Beanstalk," the children can out out the story to drum accompaniment provided by the teacher.

Two examples of dramatization (detailed later) of something that the children are likely to know about are "Growing Flowers" and "Snowman." In "Growing Flowers" children can curl up on the surface area, each representing a flower seed. To suitable accompaniment, or no accompaniment at all, the children use axial movements (rising, stretching, turning) to "grow" as flowers. They finally rise to the standing position with arms above the head.

In "snowman" the children can stand in informal order about the surface area as snowmen. To suitable musical or percussion accompaniment, (designated as the bright shining sun) they do a variety of movements that depict the snowmen melting as a result of the hot sun.

An example of a story made up by the teacher is shown in the following simulated teaching procedure in which a *parade* theme is used.

TEACHER: Boys and girls, how many of you know what a parade is?

(CHILDREN)

TEACHER: Good. How many of you have seen a parade?

(CHILDREN)

TEACHER: That's fine; most of you have seen a parade. What kinds of parades are there?

(CHILDREN)

TEACHER: On what days do we have parades?

(CHILDREN)

TEACHER: You have given several examples, and now I would like to tell you about a Fourth of July parade. This is a story about children watching a parade. In the parade was a group of soldiers. They marched along to the sound of music and the beat of a drum. Would someone like to show us how they marched? (One child demonstrates to the drum accompaniment provided by the teacher. The children then evaluate the good things the "marching soldier" did.)

TEACHER: George, because you did such a good job, you can be the head soldier and everyone will march along behind you. (The teacher accompanies the marching soldiers on the drum for a period of time and then they return to their original places.)

TEACHER: The children enjoyed watching the soldiers so much and tried to keep up with them. How could they do this? (The teacher sound several "run notes" and a child mentions that the children would have to run to keep up.)

TEACHER: That's right, Jack, can you show us how? (The child runs to the accompaniment, good points are evaluated, and then all children run for a short period of time and then return to their places.)

TEACHER: Now, boys and girls, something very interesting happened. (The teacher sounds several slow loud beats on the drum.)

TEACHER: What do you think that could have been? (Children give several suggestions such as a cannon, bass drum, etc. If none of the children suggest that it was a giant taking big steps, the teacher continues.)

TEACHER: Boys and girls, it was a giant taking great big giant steps. (The teacher goes through the same procedure as with the marching soldiers and running children, and the children move around the surface area with big giant steps to the drum accompaniment and back to their original places. The teacher can continue on with suggestions from the children or end the story at this point.)

Themes

The following stories prepared by the author provide a variety of creative dance themes. They are designed to be read to the children by the teacher and can be used with or without accompaniment. For some of the stories drum accompaniment is useful as mentioned previously when the drum depicted the hot sun as a stimulus for the melting snowmen.

SNOWFLAKES

Snow!
Snowflakes fall.
They fall down.

Down, down, down.
Around and around.
They fall to the ground.
Could you dance like snowflakes?

LITTLE BEE

Fly, fly, fly.
One, two, three.
Dance, dance, dance.
Dance Little Bee.
Buzz, buzz, buzz.
One, two, three.
Buzz, buzz, buzz.
Buzz Little Bee.
Could you dance like Little Bee?

MY BALOON

See my balloon.
It is big.
I dance with it.
I hit my balloon.
One, two, three.
There it goes.
High over me.
One, two, three.
Could you play that you have a balloon and dance with it?

THE GROWING FLOWERS

Flowers grow.
First they are seeds.
Be a seed.
Grow like a flower.
Grow and grow.
Keep growing.
Grow tall.
Now you are a flower.

Could you grow like a flower?

FALLING LEAVES

Leaves fall.
They fall from the trees.
They fall to the ground.
Fall like leaves.
Down, down, down.
Down to the ground.
Quiet leaves.
Rest like leaves.
Could you dance like falling leaves?

MR. SNOWMAN AND MR. SUN

See Mr. Snowman.
See Mr. Sun.
Mr. Snowman sees Mr. Sun.
Mr. Snowman is going.
Going, going, going.
Mr. Snowman is gone.
Be Mr. Snowman.
Could you do like Mr. Snowman?

RAGGEDY RAG DOLL

See Raggedy Rag Doll.
See Raggedy Rag Doll stand.
Watch Raggedy Rag Doll sit.
Watch her head.
Watch her arms.
Be Raggedy Rag Doll.
Sit down like Raggedy Rag Doll.
Could you be a Raggedy Rag Doll.

THE MOTOR CAR

Pretend you are a motor car.
Hum like the engine.

Hmm! Hmm! HMM!
Your feet are the wheels.
Go like a car.
Hum as you go.
Can you hum while you go like a motor car?

DANCE OF THE FAIRIES AND ELVES

It has been said that fairies and elves live in beautiful flower gardens.
On moonlight nights, the fairies and elves like to dance.
They gather on the beautiful lawn.
They dance quietly and lightly.
They dance and turn on their toes.
They are very grateful.
You can dance like fairies and elves.
The girls can be the fairies.
The boys can be the elves.
These words can help you with your dance.
Fairies and elves on tip-toe, dancing lightly to and fro.
Running, running on tip-toe, lightly, sprightly to and fro.
Swinging, swaying on tip-toe, dancing lightly to and fro.
Whirling, twirling on tip-toe, dancing lightly to and fro.
Leaping, leaping on tip-toe, lightly, lightly to and fro.
Fairies and elves on tip-toe, dancing lightly to and fro.
Could you and your friends dance like fairies and elves?

All of the ideas given above are suggestive points of departure to be taken. The imaginative teacher along with the children's assistance can develop many such ideas along these and similar lines. I highly recommend that teachers draw upon their own ingenuity and creativity to prepare creative dance stories. One of the reasons for this is paucity of published materials in this general area. In addition, teachers themselves can provide materials to meet the specific needs and interests of children in a given situation. Of course, one drawback is that preparation of such materials is a time-consuming effort and it may be more expedient to use professionaly prepared materials if they are available (for example see James H. Humphrey, *Learning to Listen and Read Through Movement*, Long Branch, N.J.: Kimbo Educational, 1974). However, it has been my experience that those teachers who have the ability and have been willing to take the time have produced amazingly creative stories using dance themes.

In writing stories using such a setting the new word load should be kept relatively low, and there should be as much repetition of these words as possible and appropriate. Sentence length and lack of complexity of sentences should be considered in keeping the level of difficulty of material within the independent understanding levels of children. Consideration should also be given to the listening values and literary merits of a story; using a character or characters in a story setting helps to develop interest and stimulates creativity in children.

SUGGESTIONS FOR TEACHING CREATIVE DANCE

With regard to teaching creative dance to children, a question often raised by beginning teachers is "How do I begin?" There are varying points of view on this, but most writers tend to agree on two major factors: (1) providing a creative environment, and (2) gaining the confidence of the children.

In my own experience I have found that these factors can be accomplished by beginning with unstructured individual interpretation in almost absolute form, i.e., the previously mentioned approach of having the children move in a way that the accompaniment makes them feel, with no teacher guidance. This approach tends to "free up" children and gets them into the spirit of participation so that they recognize the enjoyment to be derived from creative movement.

The following additional suggestions are submitted as possible points of departure that a teacher may take in providing learning experiences for children through creative dance. In following these suggestions the reader should take into account the various degrees of structuring to be considered in either individual interpretation or dramatization.

1. The teacher must recognize that in creative dance each child's

interpretation of accompaniment or a story may differ. For this reason the teacher's comments to a child should be characterized by praise and encouragement.

2. Although creative dance is essentially individual in nature, the teacher may wish to introduce it to groups of children. This helps to avoid embarrassment of children and tends to build up their self-confidence.

3. It is probably a good plan to disperse the group informally about the activity area. Formal arrangement may not always be conducive to creativity.

4. When accompaniment is used the children can listen to it for the purpose of becoming accustomed its tempo and mood. In the case of a dramatization, the teacher might introduce the activity with a rhythm or story.

5. The children should be given an opportunity to discuss the accompaniment in terms of "what it says" or "how it makes us feel."

6. The children can give their creative interpretation to the accompaniment.

7. The teacher may wish to ask some children to show their interpretations to the rest of the group. This procedure can provide a medium for evaluation.

ONE TEACHER'S APPROACH[4]

The foregoing discussions have no doubt indicated the almost unlimited possibilities inherent in creative dance for children. And, there are several outstanding creative teachers on the "firing line" carrying on these exciting teaching–learning experiences. One such person is Theresa Purcell, a physical education teacher at the Brunswick Acres Elementary School in Kendall Park, New Jersey, who has kindly agreed to share her ideas with us.

To begin with she asks us to visualize a six-year-old child running as fast as she can waving a red streamer high over her head, then

[4] Theresa, Purcell, "Creating Dances with Children: A Sharing Experience," *The Easterner*, (Indiana, Pa.), January 1986.

spinning around slowly falling to the floor with the steamer floating down beside her. In this dance phrase, the child can be expressing the excitement the color red evokes or she can be using the streamer to represent the movement of a hot red flame. For children, dancing is a wonderful way to express the natural desire to move in the environment.

Theresa Purcell contends that designing dances with children can be an enlightening experience for both teacher and student. Each student brings his own background of movement experiences and creative potential to the lesson. The teacher offers knowledge of movement and the process for creating a dance. Dances can be designed as a one-time experience or can be repeated and rehearsed for a performance. These dances should contain movements that are natural for children, yet also allow for development of their individual movement vocabulary. The role of the teacher is to guide children in exploring dance ideas and help them form movements into sequences to compose a dance. Three steps are suggested.

1. Choosing an idea to express through dance movement. This idea can be initiated by props, music, literature, movement themes, feeling, events, etc.
2. Exploring the various qualities of the idea. This will involve use of body shapes, time, space, and energy, and how these concepts relate to the idea being explored.
3. Forming the structure of the dance. This involves establishing a sequence: where and how the dance will begin, where and how the dancers will move, where and how the end of the dance will occur.

Using the decisions about content and sequence, the teacher and students work together to choreograph the dance. It is valuable for the teacher to actively participate with the students in helping them express the interpretation of the dance idea through movement.

Ms. Purcell places emphasis on *what to dance about*, or *initiating ideas*. These include:

1. *Props:* curtains, streamers, chairs, hoops, tires, tissues, scarves, balloons, ropes, paper bags, pieces of long material, balls, etc.

2. *Music:* recorded music, homemade instruments, voice, percussion instruments, and other instruments as violin, flute, piano, etc.
3. *Literature:* stories, poems, words, stories made up by students or teachers.
4. *Movement themes:* space (levels, directions, shapes, pathways, range) body awareness (body parts), time (tempo, rhythm), force (strong, light) flow (bound, free), locomotor and non-locomotor movements.
5. *Others:* feelings (happy, sad, angry, scared, etc.); events (birthdays, halloween, welcoming a new student to the class, etc.); sports, colors, names of the dancers, animals, environments (wind, outer space, under water, fire, etc.), situations (for example, dancers connected to one another, or connected to the wall or floor).

Much emphasis is given to *how to explore and develop the content of for the dance:* Exploration provides each child with the opportunity to experiment with a movement task under the careful guidance and direction of the teacher. The teacher first presents a movement task to the students, then time is allotted for the student to experiment and explore a variety of solutions using their own resources. The solution is an individual, partner or group response that falls within the confines of the stated task. While the students are working on the task, the teacher can circulate among the children in order to give reinforcement, ask questions, or add more challenges. A predetermined answer should not be considered by the teacher, rather the solution should be open to all the different student interpretations of the task. For example, exploring with red streamers the teacher may present the following tasks: "Can you find a way to move the streamer over your head as you turn around in your place?" "See if you can write your name in the air using the streamer." "Write it as fast as you can." "Try tossing and catching the streamer; can it land on a different body each time you toss it?"

Her recommendations for forming the structure of the dance involve establishing a sequence. . . . Where will the dance begin?. . . . Where and how will the dancers move?. . . . Where will the end of the dance happen?

1. Beginning places for dancers can be the perimeter of the space, corners of the space, in one or two corners, opposite sides of the space, lines in the space, scattered or circle.
2. Dancers can move toward and away from a common center, around the perimeter of the space, predetermined path (circle, spiral, zig-zag), toward a corner of side of the space, scattered, moving through the space, or remaining stationary.
3. In ending the dance, the same formations described for the beginning of the dance can also be used for the ending. Students can freeze in a shape, together or alone, end falling to the floor, or exit the space.

Finally, Ms. Purcell presents a sample lesson:

Dance Idea

PROPS: Streamers of four different colors, red, green, yellow, and blue.

EXPLORATION: Find a space in the room and try to move the streamer high and low, fast and slow. The teacher can stop the class and have different students demonstrate their ideas and the class can try them. Can you run with the streamer? What other ways can you move through the space? Skip? Gallop? Is there a way you can spin around with the streamer and hold it out from you? Try spinning low to the floor as the streamer moves up and down. The teacher may design the tasks to be very specific or more general depending upon the movement background of the students.

Structure of the Dance

Beginning place of the dance: Each color streamer will be in a different corner of the space.

Where and how the dancers will move: First, the red streamer group will skip to the center of the space, spin around, and skip back to their starting space. Then the green group does the same, and when they return to their space the blue group moves the same way, and finally the yellow group takes its turn doing the same movement. Second, the red group begins to run around the perimeter of the space holding the streamers over their head; as they pass the yellow group they follow the red group in the running . . . then the green and blue group in as the red group passes them. All the dancers then change their running pattern to a scattered formation moving quickly through the space, streamers waving in the air. The third part begins with the teacher calling for everyone to STOP, then slowly moving into a larger circle. The students all together move the steamers up high with their arm quickly and down slowly several times. On a signal by the teacher everyone throws the streamers into the air and falls to the floor with the streamers floating down beside them.

Ending the dance: Students slowly sit up from the floor and walk back to the corner where they started leaving the streamers on the floor.

(Theresa Purcell is a notable authority on creative dance for children. She has presented programs at the district and national level).

CHAPTER 8

STRUCTURED DANCE FORMS

In the first chapter, it may be recalled, I suggested that the types of dance activities provided for children would depend on the kinds of experiences that one might want children to have. At that point I recommended the use of (1) unstructured experiences, (2) semi-structured experiences and (3) structured experiences. Structured experiences were identified as those involving the more difficult dance patterns associated with various types of dances; and this comprises the content of the present chapter.

I am well aware of the fact that some dance enthusiasts have opposed the use of this form of dance, not only with children but with adults as well. The thinking seems to have been that suitable learning does not take place when this type of dance form is used. This argument is certainly acceptable in those instances where structured dance forms are "taught" incorrectly. However, if valid principles of learning are applied children can *explore* and *discover* as well through structured as through unstructured dance forms. On the other hand, if children are expected to react only "on the numbers," then the extensive use of structured dance forms might be questioned. Therefore, it does not necessarily mean that success depends on *what* is taught but *how* it is taught as well.

PROGRESSION IN STRUCTURED DANCE FORMS

As is the case with any physically-oriented activity, developing a progressive sequence of dances according to degree of difficulty is no easy matter. There are ways of doing this, however. One that I have found satisfactory is to provide for progression in terms of *organization* and *function*. Teachers can analyze dances, with reference to degree of difficulty of performance, with these two factors in mind. *Organization* refers to the degree of complexity with which the dance is executed, and *function*, to the degree of difficulty of the dance patterns.

A simple form of organization would be one in which the children are in a single circle without partners, while a more complex form of organization would involve a double circle and performing with partners. (Various forms of organization will be considered in a subsequent section of the chapter). As far as function is concerned a simple dance pattern would involve one in which only one or possibly two different, even basic, locomotor movements are performed. Dance patterns become more complex as more basic locomotor movements are used in various combinations. In the examples of dances given later in the chapter, the reader can experiment with placing them in a reasonable facsimile of sequential order of progression by using the above information for this purpose.

CLASSIFICATION OF STRUCTURED DANCES

There are many ways to classify structured dances, and usually these ways are based on the philosophy (also the whims) of the person doing the classifying. Some people like to classify structured dance forms on the basis of organization; for example, circle dances, longways dances, and the like. Others might classify them according to what is done in the dance; for example, "greeting and meeting" dances. One particular thing that needs to be taken into account, regardless of the way one tends to classify structured dances, is that there will be a certain amount of unavoidable overlapping in any classification. For instance, if a *movement song* is described as a form of dance that requires singing accompaniment, the same could be said for a *square dance* using a singing call.

Having made all of the above statements—for better or for worse—I will use the following classification for structured dances: (1) movement songs, (2) folk dances, and (3) square dances. The reader should take into account the aforementioned aspects of unavoidable overlapping. (Later in the chapter several representative examples of all of these types of dances will be described, along with suggested procedures for teaching them).

FORMATIONS FOR THE ORGANIZATION OF DANCES

Structured dances imply that there is some sort of structured formation needed to organize and perform a particular dance. Three such forms of organization will be discussed here: (1) circle, (2) longways, and (3) square. In addition, organizing with partners and organizing for dances in limited space such as the classroom will be considered.

1. *Circle.* Dances and other activities have taken place in a circle formation for as long as can be remembered. For example, in the Apocryphal New Testament *Acts of John:* "So he told us to form a circle, holding one another's hands, and he himself stood in the middle and said, 'Answer Amen to me.' " Christ is said to have bidden his disciples just prior to his arrest to form a circle and dance while he sang a hymn. It has been suggested that this account describes a ritual which a group of Gnostics actually performed. However, the early Christian Church rejected the Acts of John, and afford Christ the dancer no place in the canonical writings. Yet today some maintain that the circle dance may have been part of early Christian worship.

Some teachers feel that the circle formation has a positive psychological effect in that it tends to provide a spirit of unity among the dancers. That is, in some of these dances the participants can see and become aware of the performance of other dancers in the group.

Two types of circles are ordinarily used for dance activities—single circles and double circles. In the single circle children can stand facing inward, outward, or one behind the other depending upon how the dance is to be performed.

In some of the more complex dance patterns a double circle is employed. The same formations as the above can be used. Children in the inner circle can face those in the outer circle, both circles can face inward or outward, both circles can move clockwise or counter-clockwise, or one circle can move clockwise and the other counter-clockwise—depending upon a particular dance.

Forming a single circle of young children for the first time can be done by the teacher taking the hand of one child and then each child in turn taking the hand of another. The teacher can "circle around" and take the hand of the last child to form the circle. After the children understand the concept of a circle the teacher can ordinarily just tell them to arrange themselves in one. Circles may be made larger by each child taking a specific number of steps backward, and smaller by taking steps forward.

2. *Longways.* Dances performed from this formation are sometimes called *line* dances. However, technically, the latter term is incorrect by definition. That is, a line is an arrangement where participants stand side by side to form the line. On the other hand, when participants are one behind the other (as in the case of some longways dances) this is called a *file* or a *column.* Thus, the reason for referring to these two alignments as longways.

3. *Square.* This formation is occasionally called *quadrille,* which figuratively means "four-square." The boy is on the left and the girl is on the right.

4. *Organizing for Partners.* More often than not too much is made in the beginning in insisting on boy–girl partners. As their natural feelings toward dance evolve, this partner relationship "problem" will oftentimes take care of itself. This is to say that such a natural relationship will become acceptable because of the nature of certain kinds of dance activities.

It is doubtful whether there is any foolproof way of successfully arranging for partners. Basically, there are two general ways in which partner arrangement may be carried out—*natural* and *mechanical.* The natural way is simply to have the boys select the girls; the converse can be done in modern times with the changing attitudes toward female behavior—the girls can select the boys. There are a variety of mechanical possibilities, one of which is to form a double circle with girls on the inside circle facing the boys in the outside circle. The teacher can use a drum or a recorded musical accompaniment selection to start the circles moving, with the girls going in one direction and the boys in the other. When the accompaniment stops, the boys and girls nearest each other become partners. I once observed this procedure and noticed that in some cases either some of the boys or girls would slow down or speed up in order to avoid a particular person. Embarrassing, to say the least.

Some years ago as a beginning elementary school physical education teacher, I struck on what turned out to be a stupid idea, that of placing the girls' names in a box and having the boys draw a name. Some boys placed their hands over their eyes in doomed despair after finding out the name of the girl, and only then went over and asked the girl to be their partner—a behavior not very conducive to the girl's morale.

Sometimes at certain ages some boys consider it to be "tantamount to a commitment to marriage" if they are asked to select a girl for a dance partner. When this sort of occasion arises, the "partner problem" can be avoided by using longways dances, where there is a constant change of partners or where it is not necessary to have a partner.

5. *Organizing in Limited Space.* On occasion it may be necessary to confine dance activities to a limited area such as the regular classroom when no other space is available. At first glance this might appear impossible. Nevertheless, with wise planning and effective organization it is possible to conduct certain dance activities within the limited confines of the average classroom. This is important when the classroom teacher has responsibility for dance activities.

The way in which one organizes for classroom dance activities will depend generally upon such factors as the kinds of dance activities to be taught and the time required to arrange the room before and after activity. The following suggestions for preparing the classroom for dance activities have certain advantages and disadvantages, and for this reason the above factors need to be taken into account. In all of the following plans it is expected that a system will be devised whereby the children will be able to prepare the room effectively and efficiently under the guidance of the teacher.

1. *Clear the room of all furniture.* The obvious advantage of this plan is that it provides a maximum amount of space for activity. However, an inordinate amount of time may be required to get the furniture in and out of the room. In addition, furniture in the hall outside the room may cause an obstruction.
2. *Move furniture to one side.* This procedure will clear a little more than half the room space for activity. It has the advantage of not consuming much time for room preparation.
3. *Place furniture on all sides around the walls.* With this plan all space is available for utilization with the exception of three or four feet taken up by the furniture around the walls. An advantage of this setup is that children who are not participating due to lack of space are in a good position to observe those who are participating. With this arrangement, however, it is not always as easy to get the furniture back to its original position as quickly as when the furniture is placed at the side of the room. In this regard some plan of organization should be effected, regardless of how the room is prepared, to get children in and out of activities with little loss of time.
4. *Place furniture in center of room.* This plan is useful when circle dances are to be used if there is no need to have performers within the circle. The circle is arranged around the furniture, which does not pose an encumbrance.

DANCES INVOLVING MOVEMENT SONGS

Dances involving movement songs have traditionally been referred to as *singing games*. This designation, however, is changing, at least in the literature, where there seems to be more of a trend to refer to this form of children's dance as *movement songs,* and in some cases *action songs.* A reason advanced by Victor Dauer and Robert Pangrazi[1] as to why the term singing games is losing favor in present-day terminology is that few of the songs can accurately be called games.

Gladys Andrews Fleming[2] has characterized this type of dance as an initial form of folk dance that has been inherited by children all over the world and is deeply rooted in the heritage of ethnic groups as evidenced by their being danced generation after generation.

Movement songs are actually dances with relatively simple patterns that children perform to their own singing accompaniment or, as in the case of recorded accompaniment, when the singing is furnished by others. Some years ago Richard Kraus[3] suggested the following classification for these kinds of dances.

1. Those which enact simple stories or imitate the actions of everyday life.
2. Those which are based on familiar nursery rhymes or folktales.
3. Those which involve choosing partners.
4. Those in which children follow the leader in improvising rhythmic actions.

Several representative examples of movement songs follow. These are recommended generally for the levels from Kindergarten through Grade Two. It will be noticed that musical examples have not been included. There are two major reasons for this. First, the traditional melody for the words of most of the movement songs will already be known by many readers; and second, teachers should be encouraged to develop their own melodies. This can be done in many instances in collaboration with the children, using for instance some of the popular television commercial jingles. Second, to provide musical

[1] Victor P. Dauer and Robert P. Pangrazi, *Dynamic Physical Education for Elementary School Children,* 6th ed., (Minneapolis: Burgess Publishing Company, 1979), pp. 206–207.
[2] Gladys Andrews Fleming, *Creative Rhythmic Movement, Boys and Girls Dancing,* 2nd ed., Englewood Cliffs, N.J.: Prentice-Hall, 1976), p. 278.
[3] Richard Kraus, *A Pocket Guide of Folk and Square Dances and Singing Games for the Elementary School,* (Englewood Cliffs, N.J.: Prentice-Hall, 1966).

examples would be meaningless for those who do not read music. In addition, although it can be helpful in the teaching of movement songs for the teacher to be able to read music, this is not absolutely necessary.

A-Hunting We Will Go

Formation: Longways
Verse

1. A-hunting we will go.
2. A-hunting we will go.
3. We'll find a fox and put him in a box.
4. But then we'll let him go.

Action

Either four or six children stand in two lines, partners facing each other. The two partners nearest the front of the room should be designated as the head couple. The head couple joins hands and slides four steps down away from the front of the room between the two lines while singing the first line of the verse. The other children clap and sing the accompaniment. On the second line of the verse the head couple slides four steps back to their original position. The head couple then drops hands and the head girl skips around the right and to the end of her line. The head boy does the same thing to his left. This is done while singing the last two lines of the verse. They both meet at the other end of the line. The new head couple follows this procedure and then all succeeding couples become head couples until everyone has had an opportunity to be the head couple. After each couple has had an opportunity to be the head couple, the children all join hands and circle clockwise while singing the entire verse.

Cobbler, Cobbler

Formation: Circle
Verse 1

1. Cobbler, Cobbler.
2. Mend my shoe.
3. Have it done by
4. Half-past two.

Verse 2

5. Sew it up.
6. Sew it down.
7. Now see with whom
8. The shoe is found.

Action

The children form a large single circle with one child in the center. The child in the center holds a shoe, or an object representing a shoe. During the singing of Verse 1, the child in the center passes the shoe to another in the circle. The shoe is then passed behind the backs of the children during the singing of Verse 2. On the word "found," the child who has the shoe becomes "it" and goes to the center of the circle. This continues for as long as desired.

Did You Ever See a Lassie?

Formation: Circle
Verse

1. Did you ever see a lassie, a lassie, a lassie?
2. Did you ever see a lassie go this way and that?
3. Go this way and that way, go this way and that way.
4. Did you ever see a lassie go this way and that?

Action

The children form a circle and one child is chosen to be the leader and stands in the center. On line 3 of the Verse the leader goes through some sort of motion and the children in the circle follow. This continues with different children going to the center of the circle.

When a boy is the leader, "laddie" is substituted for "lassie." Or, if desired, the names of the child in the center can be used: "Did you ever see Richard?" etc.

d

Diddle Diddle Dumpling

Formation: Optional
Verse

1. Diddle Diddle Dumpling, my son John.
2. Went to bed with one shoe on.
3. Yes, one shoe off, and one shoe on.
4. Diddle Diddle Dumpling, my son John.

Action

The children can be in any formation. On the first line they can clap either hands, knees, or thighs, or they can do the sailor hop. (The sailor hop is done by standing with the feet together and then placing first one heel and then the other in front of the other with a short hop). On the second line they can pretend to sleep, such as placing head on hands. On the third line they hop on one foot and then on the other to indicate they have a shoe off. On the fourth line they repeat the action of the first line.

Hickory Dickory Dock

Formation: Double Circle Facing in
Verse

1. Hickory Dickory Dock.
2. The mouse ran up the clock.
3. The clock struck one!
4. Watch the mouse run!
5. Hickory Dickory Dock.

Action

The children form a double circle with partners facing. On Line 1 the hands are in front of the body to form pendulums and the arms are swung left and right. On Line 2 partners change places with six short running steps. On Line 3 they clap hands over head. On Line 4 they go back to their original place with six short running steps. On Line 5 they swing the arms as in Line 1.

Jolly is the Miller

Formation: Double Circle Facing Counterclockwise
Verse

1. Jolly is the miller who lives by the mill.
2. The wheel goes round with a right good will.
3. One hand in the hopper and the other in the sack.
4. The right skips forward and the left skips back.

Action

The children form a double circle facing counterclockwise with inside hands joined. An extra participant takes a place near the center of the circle. On Lines 1, 2, and 3 the children move in a circle by walking or skipping, stopping on the word "sack." On Line 4 partners drop hands. The children on the outside move backward one step to get a new partner whereupon the child in the center tries to get a partner. The procedure continues.

It is an interesting approach when teachers develop their own movement songs. This can be done in story form and read to the children. The following is one example of several stories that I have prepared for this purpose.

SING A SONG OF DANCING

Can you sing as you dance?
It is fun.
Here are some new words to an old song.
The song is, "Sing a Song of Sixpence."
The words tell you how to do the dance.

Sing a song of dancing
Standing in a ring.
Bow low to your partner
Smile as you sing.
Take the hand of partner
Now skip around the ring.
Isn't it a heap of fun
To skip around and sing?
Could your partner and you
skip in time to the singing?

Some Suggested Procedures for Teaching Movement Songs

The following teaching procedures are submitted as suggestive points of departure that the teacher might consider in providing learning experiences for children through movement songs.

1. The teacher can sing the entire song. Or the words of the song can be read to the children and they can attempt to provide a melody for it.
2. The teacher may wish to have the children discuss the song in terms of what it says.
3. The song can then be sung by phrases, with the teacher singing a phrase and then the children repeating the phrase.
4. The phrases can then be put together with the children singing the whole song.
5. The movement pattern that goes with the song can then be introduced using appropriate visual input, and the song and activity can be combined.
6. In cases where the movement song is long and has several verses, each verse and the activity that goes with the verse can be learned. All verses can then be combined into the whole movement song.
7. Depending upon the movement involved, movement songs can be vigorous activities for children. Because voices tend to tire when activity is engaged in while singing, it may be a wise practice not to have too many movement songs in succession. In other words,

it might be well to combine movement songs and other dance activities during the class period.

FOLK DANCES

The adjective *folk* derives from Old English and refers to the customs widely used among common people and passed on from one generation to another. Folk dances are sometimes called *nationality* or *ethnic* dances. One authorative dance source, Gertrude Blanchard,[4] has suggested that ethnic dance is a total dance culture and that folk dance is that part of ethnic dance that is performed for fun, for the joy of moving, and for the personal pleasures of interrelating with others in rhythmic patterns.

A definition of folk dance that has stood the test of years is that given by one expert in the area, the late Anne Schley Duggan:[5] Traditional dances of a given country which have evolved nationally and spontaneously in conjunction with the everyday activities and experiences of the people who developed them.

Folk dance patterns are performed in group formation and range from simple to rather complex forms. Many of the folk dances used in American elementary schools have been derived from Great Britain and Europe, although some have their origin in their own country. Several representative examples of folk dances follow. (The coded record sources will be found in detail in the Appendix).

CHILDREN'S POLKA (GERMAN)

This dance, also known as *Kinderpolka* may be misnamed because it does not involve a polka step. The children seem to like the finger pointing or scolding of the partner and will do so very vigorously.

---

[4] Gertrude Blanchard, *Children's Dance*, rev. ed., (Washington, D.C.: American Alliance for Health, Physical Education, Recreation and Dance, 1981), p. 57.
[5] Anne Schley, Duggan, et al., *The Teaching of Folk Dance*, (New York: A. S. Barnes & Company, 1948).

Record Sources: #10-1187; #19-45-6179, 2042; #23-750

Formation: Circle

In the starting position for this dance the children form a single circle. Partners turn and face each other. They join hands and extend the arms shoulder height.

Accompaniment	Action
Measures 1–2	Partners take two slides toward the center of the circle, and stomp feet three times in place—right, left, right.
Measures 3–4	Partners take two slides back to original position and stomp feet three times.
Measuresd 5–8	Repeat the action in Measures 1–4.
Measures 9–10	Clap hands against own thighs, clap own hands, and clap partner's hands three times.
Measures 11–12	Repeat the action in Measures 9–10
Measure 13	Extend the right foot to the side with the toe down. Hold the right elbow in the left hand and shake the right forefinger at partner three times.
Measure 14	Same as Measure 13 except that the position is reversed with left foot and left hand.
Measures 15–16	Each person turns around with four fast running steps and then stomps feet three times—right, left, right.

CHIMES OF DUNKIRK (FRANCE)

This dance is about the chimes of the church ringing in the town of Dunkirk. The town became well known in this country during World War II because of the evacuation of more than 300,000 Allied troops who were cut off from retreat on land by the German breakthrough to the French channel ports.

Record Sources: #10-1188; #19-45-6176, 17327

Formation: Double Circle

The starting position is a double circle with the girls making up the outside circle and the boys the inside circle.

Accompaniment	*Action*
Measures 1–2	Stomp feet three times—right, left, right.
Measures 3–4	Each person claps own hands three times with the arms extended over the head.
Measures 5–8	Partners join hands and skip around each other in place.
Measures 9–16	Partners hold inside hands and skip around the circle to either the right or left.

CSEBOGAR (HUNGARIAN)

This is a very popular Hungarian dance the name of which means the *beetle*.

The starting position is a single circle of partners with the girls on the right of their partners. All join hands.

Record Source: #19-45-6182

Formation: Circle facing in

Accompaniment	*Action*
Measures 1–4	With two slides to a measure the circle takes eight slides to the left.
Measures 5–8	Repeat of measures 1–4 but going to the right, or back to original position.
Measures 9–12	Four walking steps to the center and four walking steps back (when the circle reaches the center raise arms over head and shout, Hey!)
Measures 13–16	Do the Hungarian Turn with partner. (Partners place right hands at each other's waists raising left hands high over head and skip around partner twice).
Measures 17–20	Partners face each other and take hands extending arms shoulder high, taking four slow slides to the center with one slide to each measure.
Measures 21–24	Take four slow slides back to place.
Measures 25–26	Take two slow slides to center.
Measures 27–28	

Take two slow slides back to place.

Measures 29–32 Hungarian Turn as in Measures 13–16.

DANCE OF GREETING (DANISH)

*Record Sources:*k #10-1187; #19-45-6183; #23-726
Formation: Single Circle facing in
The starting position is a single circle of partners with the girl to the right of her partner.

Accompaniment	*Action*
Measure 1	Each person claps own hands twice and then turns and bows to partner.
Measure 2	All facing center of circle clap own hands twice and then turn and bow to neighbor.
Measure 3	Stomp right foot and then left foot.
Measure 4	Turn all the way around in place with short running steps.
Measures 5–8	Join hands in single circle and skip to the right.

PAW PAW PATCH (AMERICAN)

Record Sources: #10-1181; #19-45-5066
Formation: Longways
In the starting position there are several couples. Boys stand one behind the other in one column and the girls in the other, all facing in the same direction.

Verse

1. Where, or where is pretty little Mary? (Actual name can be substituted.)
   Where, or where is pretty little Mary?
   Where, or where is pretty little Mary?
   Way down yonder in the paw paw patch.
2. Come on boys, let's go find her.
   Come on boys, let's go find her.

Come on boys, let's go find her.
Way down yonder in the paw paw patch.
3. Pickin' up paw paws, put 'em in your pocket.
Pickin' up paw paws, put 'em in your pocket.
Pickin' up paw paws, put 'em in your pocket.
Way down yonder in the paw paw patch.

On verse 1 the girl at the head of her column turns to the right and skips around the whole group and back to her original place. All others stay in place and clap their hands and sing. On verse 2 the first girl again turns to her right and does the same thing as she did in verse 1. However, this time she is followed by all in the boys' column. On verse 3 partners take inside hands and skip around in a circle. When the head couple is at the end of the column, they form an arch while the other couples skip back to the original position. There is now a new head couple and the same procedure is continued until all have gone through the entire dance.

A popular form of folk dances, most of which have had their origin in America, are *mixers*. Many children like mixers because they provide for constant change of partners. An example follows.

GLOW WORM MIXER (AMERICAN)

Record Sources: #10-E1158; #27-4613
Formation: Circle of partners facing counterclockwise
In the starting position a double circle of partners taking hands stand facing counterclockwise. Girls are on the right.

Accompaniment	*Action*
Measure 1	Starting on the left foot, all take four steps forward.
Measure 2	Partners release hands and face each other. The boys take four steps backward away from the center.
Measure 3	All walk forward four steps diagonally to the left, and meet a new partner.
Measure 4	Taking both hands of the new partner each couple

turns clockwise one time with four steps. They are now facing counterclockwise and the dance is repeated for the duration of the accompaniment.

SQUARE DANCES

Square dancing appears to be uniquely American in origin. It is sometimes referred to as American country dancing or Western dancing. The square dance gets its name from the starting position of the dancers which is that of a quadrille or square. Square dancing is done to musical accompaniment with a *caller* who gives cues as to what the dance patterns are.

There are three general calls for square dancing: (1)l the *prompt* call, (2) the *patter* call, and (3) the *singing* call. The prompt call involves simple and precise commands. This type of call is not done to a melody or rhyme. Calls are given and the caller waits until the steps are executed and then gives the next call. This call may be used in preparation to do patter calling since it is easier than patter calling. Patter calling is done by chanting or a singsong fashion and generally in rhyme. The amount of time for each patter call is the same as the number of beats necessary to do a particular step or pattern that is called. The singing call is essentially the same as the patter call except that it is done to the melody of a particular song.

With practice, children as well as the teacher can become reasonably proficient at calling. Although there is a difference of opinion as to what type of call to use for beginners, my own personal experience has been to use the singing call. The reason that I have found for this is that the caller need not count the number of beats which is necessary in prompt and patter calling.

The following are representative of some of the square dances utilizing singing calls that have been used with success at the elementary school level. Although for the most part, square dancing is ordinarily done at the intermediate level, it is possible to do it at a lower level depending upon the skill of the teacher and the complexity of the dance patterns.

PIG IN THE PARLOR

This dance involves a singing call which is sung to the tune of "For He's a Jolly Good Fellow."
Call
1. There is a pig in the parlor,
2. There is a pig in the parlor,
3. There is a pig in the parlor,
4. And he is fat and round.
5. Your right hand to your partner.
6. Your left hand to your neighbor.
7. Back again to your partner,
8. And swing her round and round.

Action

On Lines 1–4 all members of the square join hands and circle around to the right returning to their original positions. On Line 5 partners do an *allemande right* (which means to the right hand). This is done by grasping right hands and completing a circle by walking all the way around the partner and back to original position. On Line 6 an *allemande left* is performed. This is just the opposite of the allemande right with the boy taking the left hand of the girl on his left (his corner or neighbor). On Lines 7–8 an elbow swing is performed with the partner. This is done by interlocking elbows and skipping around in a circle one or more times. (If there is an extra person, he or she can stand in the center of the square and try to get a partner just before the elbow swing. The person whose partner is "stolen" then becomes the pig).

RED RIVER VALLEY

The singing call for this dance is sung to the tune of "Red River Valley."
Call

1. Now you all join hands in the valley.

2. And you circle to the left and to the right.
3. And now you swing that girl in the valley.
4. Now you swing with your Red River girl.
5. First couple lead to the valley.
6. And you circle to the left and to the right.
7. And now you swing the girl in the valley.
8. Now you swing with the Red River girl.
9. Now all of you go to the center.
10. And all of you come right back out again.
11. Now you skip with your partner around the circle,
12. Until you get back home once again.

Action

On Lines 1–2 everyone joins hands and walks four steps to the right and then reversing this procedure with four steps to the left. On Line 3 boys swing the girl on their left. On Line 4 all boys swing their own partner. On Lines 5–6 the First Couple moves to the Second Couple. Both couples join hands and walk in a circle four steps to the right and then reverse with four steps to the left. On Line 7 the boys in Couple One and Two swing opposite girls. On Line 8 boys swing own partner.

This is what is known as a *Visiting Couple Dance* and after the First Couple has visited the Second Couple they go on and visit the Third and Fourth Couples. In doing this the dance patterns in Lines 5–8 are repeated. The Second, Third, and Fourth Couples visit around the square in the same manner as the First Couple. They each do this in turn and the dance patterns in Lines 5–8 are repeated each time.

On Line 9 all join hands and walk four steps in to the center raising hands as they go. On Line 10 four steps are taken back and hands are lowered. On Lines 11–12 all partners join inside hands and skip around the square and back to their original place.

OH JOHNNY

The singing call for this dance is sung to the tune of "Oh Johnny." *Record Source:* #10-1037

Call

1. Now you all join hands and you circle the ring.
2. When you get back home you give your partner a swing.

3. Swing your neighbor girl right behind you.
4. Now swing your own so that she won't be alone.
5. It's allemande left with your neighbor girl.
6. Now back and swing your own.
7. Skip all around with your own partner bound.
8. Singing Oh Johnny, Oh Johnny, Oh.

Action

On Line 1 all join hands and circle to the right and back to original position. On Line 2 boys swing their partners. On Line 3 boys swing the girl on their left. On Line 4 boys swing partners again. On Line 5 boys do an allemande left with the girls on the left by taking hands and walking all around each other. On Line 6 boys swing own partners. On Lines 7–8, holding inside hands, partners skip around the circle and back to their places.

As in movement songs it is an interesting approach when teachers develop their own square dance calls. This can be done in story form and can be placed in the hands of children or at the lower levels read to them. The following example is one of several stories that I have prepared for this purpose.

THE YANKEE DOODLE DANCE

We all like to sing "Yankee Doodle."
Do you know the tune?
I know a dance we can do.
Here is how we do it.
We need groups of eight.
There are four partners in each group.
Each set of partners is called a couple.
One couple is the Head Couple.
The Second Couple stands to their right.
The Third Couple stands facing the First Couple.
The Fourth Couple stands facing the Second Couple
This looks like a square.

The girl on the boy's right is his partner.
Try to learn these words to the tune of Yankee Doodle.
Here is the first part.

We circle left, we circle left,
We circle left and, mind you,
Now don't forget to swing that girl,
The girl you left behind you.
Here is the second part.
Take your partner by the hand,
And walk with her around, sir.
Now you swing her arm in arm,
And sit right down beside her.
Put both parts together.
Sing as you do the whole dance.

Some Suggested Procedures for Teaching Folk and Square Dances

The following teaching procedures are submitted as suggested points of departure that the teacher may take in providing learning experiences for children through folk and square dances.

1. The name of the dance should be given. If the teacher knows where the dance got its name, and this seems important to the learning situation, the teacher can give this information to the children.
2. If the teacher feels that it is important to the learning situation, the background of the dance can be given with respect to the culture of the people who previously danced it, when they danced it, and for what purpose.
3. The introductory discussion of the dance (auditory input) should not be so intense and involved that it detracts from actual participation in the dance. It should be remembered that the greatest appreciation is likely to come from engaging in the dance.
4. Have the children listen to the accompaniment to become acquainted with the tempo and mood. Give them an opportunity to discuss the accompaniment.
5. Introduce the various movement patterns using appropriate auditory and visual input. Give the children an opportunity to practice the patterns.

6. Teach one part of the dance at a time, adding each part after the preceding part is learned. This procedure will depend to some extent upon the length and complexity of the dance. If it is short the children may be able to learn the entire dance. (Teaching by counting or phrasing, or a combination of the two, should be optional with the individual teacher.)

7. All the parts and accompaniment should be put together into the whole dance.

CHAPTER 9

HOW CHILDREN CAN LEARN ABOUT READING THROUGH DANCE ACTIVITIES

In Chapter 4 I introduced my concept of cognitive dance, explaining that this involves the use of dance as a learning medium in other curriculum areas. The present chapter and the following one will take into account how dance can be used to help children learn in the areas of reading and mathematics.

Deploring the fact that the cognitive dimension of dance has been slighted, one of my collaborators on another dance project, Judith Lynne Hanna[1] cites such old proverbs as "The greater the fool the better the dancer," "Never was a good dancer a good scholar," and "Good dancers have mostly better heels than heads." She refutes this by suggesting that cognition is in action whether the dancer's purpose is to work with the structure and style of movement, to visualize ideas, or to enact stories. What the dancer does is similar to the writer/speaker who manipulates words into sentences, paragraphs, and pages for style or presenting an analysis or story.

It is the express purpose of Chapters 9 and 10 to show the contri-

[1]Judith Lynne Hanna, "The Mentality and Matter of Dance," *Art Education*, (March 1983,) pp. 42†46.

bution of dance activities in facilitating learning for children and thus to extol the cognitive merits of dance.

THE LANGUAGE ARTS CURRICULUM

One of the very important areas in the education of elementary school chilaren is the language arts program. This program includes listening, speaking, reading, and writing, all of which are concerned with communication. The major purpose of the language arts is to facilitate communication.

Speaking and writing are sometimes referred to as the *expressive* phases of language, while listening and reading are considered the *receptive* phases. This implies that through speaking and writing the individual has the opportunity to express his or her own thoughts and feelings to others. Through reading and listening the individual receives the thoughts and feelings of others. Incidentally, it has been suggested that dancers have the capacity to communicate abstract concepts, to project experience extrinsic to themselves, to alter feelings and thought, and to create symbols and spheres for sending messages; as in language, cognitive processes in dance undergird the communication of feelings and ideas through symbols.[2]

Although I have indicated that the language arts program contains listening, speaking, reading, and writing, this should not be interpreted to mean that these are regarded as entirely separate entities. On the contrary, they are closely interrelated, and each can be considered as a component part of the broad area of communication. Such areas of study as spelling, word meanings, and word recognition are involved in each of the four areas.

The importance of the interrelationship of the various language arts can be shown in different ways. For example, children must use words in speaking and find them meaningful before they can read them successfully. Also, they can spell better words that they read with understanding and that they want to use for their own purposes.

[2]Ibid

In addition, their handwriting even improves when they use it in purposeful and meaningful communication, as when someone they like is going to read it. Perhaps the two most closely interrelated and interdependent phases of the language arts are listening and reading. In fact, most reading specialists agree that learning to listen is the first step in learning to read. (This relationship will be apparent in some of the subsequent discussions in the chapter.)

The modern school gives a great deal of attention to this interrelationship of the various phases of the language arts. This is reflected in the way in which language experiences are being provided for children in the better-than-average school. In the traditional elementary school it was a common practice to treat such aspects of the language arts as reading, writing, and spelling as separate subjects. As a result, they became more or less isolated and unrelated entities, and their full potential as media of expression probably was never fully realized. In the modern elementary school, where children have more freedom of expression and, consequently, greater opportunity for self-expression, the approach to teaching language arts is one that relates the various language areas to particular areas of interest. All of the phases of language arts are thus used in the solution of problems in all curriculum areas. This procedure is primarily based upon the assumption that skill in communication should be developed in all of the activities engaged in by children. *Think of the possibilities of dance!*

I have already pointed out that through reading the individual receives the thoughts and feelings of others, and that reading is considered a receptive phase of language. In this case the word *receptive* might well carry a figurative as well as a purely literal meaning: reading has indeed been on the "receiving end" of a great deal of criticism during the past few years. Perhaps more criticism has been directed at it than at all of the other subjects combined. Although it may be difficult to determine precisely why reading has suffered the brunt of attack, one could speculate that it might be because, in general, most people consider reading the real test of learning. In fact, in the early days of American education, grade levels tended to be thought of as "readers"; that is, a child was said to be in the "first reader," "second reader," and so on.

In modern times a good bit of the controversy involving reading seems to center around two general areas. First, there has been criticism of the various methods of teaching reading, and second, there has been some question regarding the validity of the principles upon which these methods are based. Perhaps, because of children's individual differences, no method used in absolute form to the exclusion of all other methods would meet the needs of all. For this reason it seems logical to assume that the procedures or combination of procedures employed should be those that best meet the needs of an individual child or a particular group of children. In this regard I have found that many children seem to learn well in the area of reading when the dance medium is used for this purpose.

It is not my purpose here to evaluate any of the past or present methods of teaching reading. Rather, the discussions in this chapter are intended to show how dance experiences can be used to assist the child in his or her efforts to read. However, before getting directly into learning about reading through dance activities, it seems appropriate to discuss certain general aspects of the area of reading, and the following comments are intended for this purpose.

THE NATURE OF READING

Practically all of us learn to read, but of course with varying degrees of proficiency. Yet, to define exactly what reading means is not an easy task. Part of the reason for this is that it means different things to different people. It has been suggested that the psychologist thinks of reading as a thought process. Those who deal in semantics, which is a study of meanings, think of reading as the graphic representation of speech. The linguist, one who specializes in speech and language, is concerned with the structure of language, its sounds, and its written form. Finally, the sociologist is concerned with the interaction of reading and culture.

I have already indicated that reading is an aspect of communication. As such, reading becomes more than just the ability to recognize a word on a printed page. To communicate, a meaning must be shared and the reader must be able to comprehend. Thus, one of the most important concerns in teaching reading is that of helping children develop comprehension skills. (Later in the chapter the matter of comprehension skills in relation to dance will be taken into account.)

Reading could be thought of as bringing meaning *to* the printed page instead of only gaining meaning *from* it. This means that the author of a reading selection does not necessarily convey ideas to the reader, but stimulates him to construct them out of his own experiences. (This is one of the major purposes of my program called the AMAV Technique, which will be dealt with in detail later in the chapter.)

Since reading is such a complex act and cannot be easily defined, I will resort to a rather broad and comprehensive description of the term. My description of reading is an *interpretation of written or printed verbal symbols*. This can range from graffiti on school restroom walls to the Harvard Classics.

It should be borne in mind that the entire child reads; he reads with his senses, his experiences, his cultural heritage, and of course with his muscles. It is the latter aspect with which we are predominantly concerned here, because the aspect of "muscle sense" involved in dance activities is an extremely important dimension in reading for children.

WHEN TO BEGIN READING INSTRUCTION

Traditionally, the practice has been to begin the teaching of reading when children enter first grade at about six years of age. However, in recent years there has been a great sentiment for starting the instruction earlier. Part of the reason for this is a general feeling that young children are becoming more mature and possess more experience at an earlier age than was the case in the past. As a result of this prevailing belief, fully one-third of the teachers at the kindergarten level feel that their children can benefit from various forms of reading instruction. In fact a large majority of kindergarten teachers conduct some of the fundamental phases of reading instruction, and only about 20 percent of them do not believe that reading instruction should be a part of the school program at that level.

A question to raise is: Does early reading instruction have any value? Completely solid evidence to support one position or another is lacking, and it is impossible to make an unqualified conclusion. One very important consideration is whether or not early instruction benefits the child as far as his or her total development is concerned. Some child development specialists feel that such instruction, if too highly structured and formalized, can actually cause harm to the emotional development and social adjustment of some children. One of the glorious features of using the dance activity learning medium to teach reading is its lack of formality and the application of creative and spontaneous experiences that are so important to the total developmental process.

READING READINESS

Closely allied to the problem of when to begin reading instruction is the question of reading readiness. There are certain *developmental tasks* that are important for children to accomplish, and reading can be considered such a developmental task. That is, it is a task that children need to perform to satisfy their personal needs as well as those requirements which society and the culture impose upon them. In viewing reading as a developmental task, we can then consider reading readiness as a developmental *stage* at which certain factors have prepared the child for reading.

At one time, reading readiness was considered only a question as to whether the child was ready to *begin* the reading experience. In more recent years it has come to be thought of more in terms of each step of reading instruction, as to readiness for the next step. Therefore, the idea of reading readiness is not confined only to the start of reading instruction, but to the teaching and learning of nearly all reading skills. A given child may be considered ready to *learn to read* at a certain age. However, this same child may not necessarily be ready to *read to learn* until a later time. In fact, some reading specialists consider the primary level of grades one through three as a time for learning to read, and the intermediate level of grades four through six as a time when the child begins to read to learn.

Reading readiness needs to be thought of as a complex combination of basic abilities and conditions and not only as a single characteristic. This combination includes (1) various aspects of visual ability, (2) certain factors concerned with the auditory sense, (3) sex differences, (4) age, and (5) socioeconomic conditions. Obviously, it not my intention here to go into detail with reference to these various characteristics, but merely to identify them. Later in the chapter specific recommendations will be made concerning the application and function of dance activities as a medium for dealing with certain aspects of the reading process.

READING AND THE DANCE EXPERIENCE

The theory that there is a high degree of relationship between participating in pleasurable movement experiences (such as dancing) and reading is not new. For example, Fénelon, the famous French educator (1651–1715) is reputed to have suggested that he had seen certain children who learned to read while playing.[3] Although I am not exactly sure what he meant, I am willing to speculate, or perhaps more accurately to rationalize, that his statement might well have been one of the first indications that there is a high level of compatibility between reading and dance activities, and a possible forerunner of some of the things I will expound in this chapter.

In any event, in more modern times many tend to believe that the *kinesthetic* sense—the sense of "feel" that children get through their muscles in enjoyable movement—seems to be highly developed, and it helps them remember words they would take much longer to learn by looking at or sounding out. Moreover, practically all modern educators subscribe to the notion that children will learn more easily if the subject matter is something in which they are personally involved.

[3]George Ellsworth Johnson, *Education by Plays and Games*, (Boston: Ginn and Company, 1907), p. 31.

Without question, dance experiences can be important to many children and "are something that they are personally involved in." Consequently, reading that uses the medium of dance as a motivating factor can be very appealing to children. Subsequent discussions in the chapter will take some of these specific kinds of experiences into account.

Using Dance Activities for Reading Instruction

Dance activities in reading instruction can serve one very important purpose. That is, they can be particularly useful for developing specific language or reading concepts. In these activities the learner acts out the concept and thus is able to visualize as well as get the "feel" of the concept.

After a dance activity has been performed, it should be evaluated not only in terms of the children's reaction to it and how it was performed, but also in terms of how well the children understand the concept inherent in the dance activity; that is, what specific reading skill they were practicing. The following illustrations describe two representative examples of how to develop a concept that is inherent in the dance activity. In the first situation the dance activity should facilitate the understanding of certain vocabulary words through performance in the activity. There has been some previous experience with the meaning of these words as well as auditory, and for some children, visual recognition of the words and the concept of opposites. The concept is *vocabulary meaning—word opposites.*

I'M TALL, I'M SMALL

The children form a circle with one child in the center. The child in the center of the circle stands with eyes closed. It may be helpful to have the child blindfolded. The children in the circle walk around the circle singing the following verse. (The children with the help of the teacher can make up a melody.)

I'm tall, I'm very small,

I'm small, I'm very tall,
Sometimes I'm tall,
Sometimes I'm small,
Guess what I am now.

As the children walk and sing "tall," "very tall," or "small," "very small," they stretch up or stoop down, depending on the words. At the end of the singing the teacher signals the children in the circle to assume a stretching or stooping position. The child in the center, still with eyes closed, guesses which position they have taken. The activity continues with another child in the center.

This activity helps children to develop word meaning by acting out the words. Use of word opposites in this manner helps to dramatize the differences in the meaning of words. The words and actions can be changed to incorporate a larger number of opposites, for example,

My hands are near, my hands are far.
Now they're far, now they're near.
Sometimes they're near.
Sometimes they're far.
Guess what they are now.

The following is a simplified teching–learning situation for this activity.

TEACHER: Boys and girls, do you remember the other day we were talking about things that were tall and things that were small? What are some of the things we found at school that were tall? (CHILDREN.) Very good, Can you think of some things we thought were small? (CHILDREN.) Can you remember some things we decided were sometimes tall and sometimes small? (CHILDREN.) That's right. We said trees could be tall and small. And we said people were both tall and small. Who in your family is tall? (CHILDREN.) And who is small? (CHILDREN.) Very good. Today we are going to do a little dance called "I'm Tall, I'm Small." We are going to need to remember what the words "tall" and "small" mean in order to do this dance. (The teacher goes over the procedures and answers any questions that children may have. During the activity the teacher may make comments.) Make sure you stretch really tall, now, boys and girls. Some of you need to get down lower when you stoop. And be sure to watch my signal at the end of the song so you will all do the same thing. All right. Let's continue.

The activity continues for a time, and then the teacher evaluates with the class.

TEACHER: What did you like best about the dance? (CHILDREN.) Is it easier to remember what the word "tall" means? (CHILDREN.) What do you think of when someone says the word "tall"? (CHILDREN). How about the word "small"? What do you think of? (CHILDREN.) How did the dance help you remember what each word means? (CHILDREN.) How could we improve the dance? (CHILDREN.) Yes, you have to watch me closely so you will carry out the right signal. Next time we do it I am going to use the word cards saying "tall" and "small" instead of signaling with my hands. (In this case the teacher will be using visual input instead of auditory input.) Do you think you could read the words so you would know whether to stretch or stoop? (CHILDREN.) Good. Will that be fun to try? (CHILDREN.)

In the second illustration the concept is *vocabulary meaning—action words*. A child can be selected as the leader and stands a short distance away from the other children who are in a line.

WHAT TO PLAY

The children sing the following verse to the tune of "Mary Had a Little Lamb."

(Name of child) tell us what to play,
What to play, what to play,
(Name) tell us what to play,
Tell us what to play.

The leader can then say "Let's play we're fishes," or Let's wash dishes," or any other thing that depicts action. The children create the action. This activity gives children an opportunity to act out meanings of words. It helps them to recognize that spoken words represent actions of people as well as things that can be touched. These examples should give the reader an idea of the possibilities of using dance activities for reading instruction. I am sure that creative teachers will be able to think of numerous others.

Dance Reading Content

The term *reading content* is easy to describe because it is simply concerned with the information that a given reading selection contains. Therefore, dance reading content provides for reading material that is oriented to dance situations. Stories of different lengths can be prepared for various readability levels, and the content focuses upon any aspect of dance, creative or structured forms.

In my work with dance reading content I have found that: (1) when a child is self-motivated and interested, he reads. In this case, the reading is done without the usual motivating devices such as picture clues and illustrations; (2) these dance stories are found to be extremely successful in stimulating interest in reading and at the same time improving a child's ability to read; and (3) because the material for these dance stories is scientifically selected, prepared, and tested, it is unique in the field of children's independent reading material. The outcomes have been most satisfactory in terms of children's interest in reading content of this nature as well as motivation to read.

From Listening to Reading

Before getting directly into the use of dance reading content, I want to take into account the important relationship between listening and reading. An important thing to remember is that the comprehension skills for listening are the same as the comprehension skills for reading. (See list of comprehension skills as they pertain to dance activities later in the chapter). The essential difference in these two receptive phases of language is in the form of *input* that is used. That is, listening is dependent upon the *auditory* (hearing) sense, and reading is dependent upon the *visual* (seeing) sense. Since the main goal of reading is comprehension, it is important to recogize that as children listen to dance situations and react to them, they are developing essential skills for reading.

This brings us to the important question, "Should teachers and other adults read to children?" People who spend their time studying about this reply with an unqualified affirmative. That is, there seems to be solid evidence to support the idea that reading to children improves their vocabulary knowledge, reading comprehension, interest in reading, and the general quality of language development. I emphasize this at this point, because we shall see later that reading to children is an important dimension in the use of dance reading content.

The AMAV Technique

My procedure for learning to read through the use of dance reading content is identified as the *AMAV Technique,* several examples of which will be presented later. The AMAV Technique involves a learning sequence from auditory input to some form of dance movement to auditory-visual input, as depicted in the following diagram:

Auditory   Movement   Auditory-Visual

Essentially, this technique is a procedure for working through dance activities to develop comprehension first in listening and then in reading. The A   M aspect of AMAV is a directed listening-thinking activity. Children first receive the thoughts and feelings expressed in a dance story through the auditory sense by listening to the story read by the teacher. Following this, the children engage in the dance experience inherent in the story, and thereby demonstrate understanding of and reaction to the story. By engaging in the dance experience, the development of comprehension becomes a part of the child's physical reality.

After the dance experience in the directed listening–thinking activity, the children move to the final aspect of the AMAV Technique,

(A-V), a combination of auditory and visual experience, by listening to the story read by the teacher and *reading along* with the teacher and other children. In this manner, comprehension is brought to the reading experience.

Although the sequence of listening to reading is a natural one, bridging the gap to the point of handling the verbal symbols required in reading poses various problems for many children. One of the outstanding features of the AMAV Technique is that the dance experience helps to serve as a bridge between listening and reading by providing direct purposeful experience for the child through dance activity after listening to the story.

Following are several examples of stories that can be used in applying the AMAV Technique. Remember, first you read the story to the children, then with various degrees of guidance they participate in the dance experience, and then you and the children read the story together. This technique is useful with children who are encountering some difficulties with comprehension, and it can be used to help a child gain some sight words and develop listening skills. As far as the latter is concerned, I have had some very successful experiences with four to five year old children, finding that many of them can retain what they have listened to for a minimum of one week and sometimes even much longer.

WE DANCE

We hold hands.
We make a ring.
We swing our arms.
We swing.
We swing.
We take four steps in.
We take four steps out.
We drop our hands.
We turn about.
Could you do this dance?

CLAP AND TAPE

I clap with my hands.
Clap, clap, clap.
I tap with my foot.
Tap, tap, tap.
I point my toe.
And around I go.
Clap, clap, clap.
Tap, tap, tap.
Could you do this dance with a friend?

SWING AROUND

Do you know the song,
  "Mary Had a Little Lamb"?
There are other words to this tune.
Sing these words.
They will tell you what to do.
Get a partner.
Take your partner's hand.
All sing these words to the same tune
  as "Mary Had a Little Lamb."
Do what the words say.
  Walk with partners round and round.
  Walk around, walk around.
  Swing your partner round and round.
  Swing and swing around.
  Skip with partner round and round.
  Skip around, skip around.
  Swing your partner round and round.
  Swing and swing around.
Could you learn these words and then do the
dance with a partner?

AROUND THE RING

Do you know a song about hunting?
It is called, "A-Hunting We Will Go."

Here is one way to do it.

Children, hold hands in a ring.

Sing these words.

Sing them like you would sing,
"A-Hunting We Will Go."
Oh! Around the ring we go.
Around the ring we go.
We stop right here.
We clap our hands.
And then sit down just so.

Have one child stand in the center.

At the end of the song all children sit down.

Sit down before you are tapped by the child
in the center.

Try not to be tapped.

Let's try it.

Could you make a ring with other children and
sing while you do this dance.

GOING TO SCHOOL

"Here We Go Round the Mulberry Bush" is fun.

Here are new words to this music.

Sing the words.

Can you dance as you sing this song?
This is the way we walk to school.
Walk to school.
Walk to school.
This is the way we walk to school.
So merrily each morning.
This is the way we run to school.
Run to school.
Run to school.
This is the way we run to school.
So merrily each morning.
This is the way we hop to school.
Hop to school.

This is the way we hop to school.
So merrily each morning.
This the way we skip to school.
Skip to school.
Skip to school.
This is the way we skip to school.
So merrily each morning.
Could you show your friends this dance?

FIND YOUR PARTNER

Do you like Christmas songs?
I like one called, "Jingle Bells."
I know some words you could sing to the
    tune of "Jingle Bells."
You could do a dance as you sing the song.
This is the way to do it.
Have two circles.
Girls form a circle on the outside.
Boys form a circle on the inside.
Each boy has a girl for a partner.
Remember your partner
When you start to sing the song, begin to walk.
Boys will walk one way around the circle.
Girls will walk the other way.
At the end of the song, find your partner.
When you do, take hands and both stoop down.
Try not to be the last one down.
This is the song.
Remember to sing it to the tune of "Jingle Bells."
Walk around, walk around.
Walk around the ring.
Oh, what fun it is to walk around the ring and sing.
Look around, look around.
Look around the town.
Find your partner when you can and everyone
    stoop down.

Maybe some children could sing while others dance.
Could you learn the song to the tune of "Jingle
Bells" and do the dance with other children?

A CIRCLE DANCE

Have you heard the tune, "Pop Goes the Weasel"?
Find other children who know the tune.
Join hands and make a circle.
Here are some words to sing to the tune.
of "Pop Goes the Weasel."
Do what the words say.

Now here we go around the ring.
And now we stop together.
And now we walk to the center of the ring.
Just like birds of a feather.
We now step back and stomp one foot.
And all turn round together.
We all join hands and circle again.
In any kind of weather.

Could you show some friends how to do this dance?

The AMAV Technique need not be applied with children who have
the ability to read a given selection. In such cases the dance reading
content, while enriching and extending the child's experiences, reinforces his or her general ability to read on his own. A child or group
of children may read a story individually, in buddy teams, or as a
group with the teacher providing individual help with words when
needed. After reading the story the children participate in the dance.
They may then reread the story and discuss how they might improve
upon their first attempt at carrying out the dance activity. With this
procedure a child is able to develop cognitive processing skills through
the physical reality of dance movements involved. The child is therefore provided opportunities to practice and maintain skills necessary
for meaningful reading.

An important aspect of dance stories is the purpose-setting and
problem-solving nature of the reading activities. The child is reading

to find out how to do something—perform a dance. The child is using all his skills in reading to solve the problem of performing the task described in the story. Both purpose-setting and problem-solving have been identified as essential to the higher cognitive processes in mature reading. Such reading activities as dance stories can provide children their first opportunities to exercise these skills with physically real experiences. Furthermore, this approach enables a teacher to assess the child's vocabulary development and how well comprehension skills are being practiced because the children actually demonstrate their understanding of what they read. Thus, the teacher can observe by their actions the children's comprehension of the material.

Dance and Comprehension Skills

As important as sight vocabulary and word analysis skills are in reading, the "bottom line" is comprehension. Without it, reading is reduced simply to the "calling of words." Many people have difficulty defining comprehension as it applies to reading. I like to think of it as the process of correctly associating meaning with word symbols, or more simply, of extracting meaning from the written or printed page. Comprehension also involves evaluation of this meaning, sorting out the correct meaning, and organizing ideas as a selection is read. In addition, there should be retention for these ideas for possible use or reference in some future endeavor.

To accomplish comprehension as described here, it is important for children to develop certain comprehension skills. The following is a list of such *general* comprehension skills along with how a teacher might evaluate how well such listening and/or reading comprehension skills are being developed through dance reading content.

1. *Getting facts.* Does the child understand what to do and how to do it?
2. *Selecting main ideas.* Does the child use succinct instructions in preparing for and doing the dance activity?
3. *Organizing main ideas by enumeration and sequence.* Does the child know the order in which the activity is performed?

4. *Following directions.* Does the child proceed with the activity according to the precise instructions in the story?
5. *Drawing inferences.* Does the child seem to draw reasonable conclusions as shown by the way he performs in the activity?
6. *Gaining independence in word mastery.* Does the child use word analysis to get a word without asking for help? (This applies only if the child has been introduced to word analysis skills.)
7. *Building a meaningful vocabulary.* Does the child use any of the words in the dance story in his speaking vocabulary as he proceeds in the dance experience?
8. *Distinguishing fact from fantasy.* Does the child indicate which stories are real and which are imaginary, particularly as far as some of the characters are concerned?

It should be recognized that different children will develop comprehension skills at different rates. Therefore, the teacher should provide cheerful guidance as needed in assisting the child in performing the dance experiences depicted in the stories.

CHAPTER 10

HOW CHILDREN CAN LEARN ABOUT MATHEMATICS THROUGH DANCE ACTIVITIES

The subject of mathematics in today's elementary schools, with the never-ending attempts at new methods and changes in content is, to say the least, bewildering. Over the years there have been many periods of change in mathematics in schools, and believe it or not, there was a time when mathematics was not even considered a proper subject of study for children. For example, in the very early days of this country the ability to compute was regarded as appropriate for a person doing menial work, but such skill was not viewed as appropriate for the aristocracy. Accordingly, the study of mathematics was not emphasized in the early schools of America, not even the study of arithmetic.[1]

For a good portion of the 19th century, much of the arithmetic taught at the grade-school level was characterized by large numbers

---

[1] In the early 1960s the subject of arithmetic became more generally known as "elementary school mathematics." No doubt the reason for this was that at about this time elementary schools were beginning to include more advanced forms of the mathematical processes in addition to the traditional study of arithmetic. The latter is concerned with numbers and the computation with them and is considered to be a branch of the broader area of mathematics.

of drill exercises. This was also accompanied by the false notion that the study of arithmetic was useful in "training the mind." It is not surprising that mathematics was viewed by large numbers of children as something to be dreaded, for exercises were deliberately designed to be difficult so as to better "exercise" the mind.

It is questionable whether today's instruction in mathematics has completely recovered from the accompanying dread of arithmetic and the idea that "difficult is good" and "fun must be bad." In fact, the school subject that appears most stressful to the greatest majority of students is mathematics. This condition prevails from the study of arithmetic upon entering school through the required courses in mathematics in college. It has become such a problem in recent years that there is now an area of study called "Math Anxiety" that is receiving increasing attention.

Perhaps an essential difference between the traditional and modern approach to the teaching of mathematics is that the latter is concerned with number concept development in *concrete* rather than *abstract* situations. The use of dance activities in learning about mathematics embraces this idea to the extent that the concrete learning situation is fully and completely realized. This is made possible because the dance learning activities are pleasurable physical activities in which the child actually engages in order to learn.

USING DANCE ACTIVITIES TO DEVELOP MATHEMATICS CONCEPTS

There are various ways in which dance activities can be used to help children develop mathematics concepts. The two illustrations that follow are representative examples of the numerous possibilities. The first illustration involves a movement song, *Ten Little Indians*. In this activity the children form a circle, all facing in. Ten children are selected to be Indians, and numbered from one to ten. As the song is sung the child whose number is called skips to the center of the circle. When ten little Indians are in the center the song is reversed. Again, each child leaves the center and returns to the circle as his number is called. Other children may become Indians, and the song is repeated. The words to the song are:

One little, two little, three little Indians,
Four little, five little, six little Indians,
Seven little, eight little, nine little Indians,
Ten little Indian boys (or girls).
Ten little, nine little, eight little Indians,
Seven little, six little, five little Indians,
Four little, three little, two little Indians,
One little Indian boy.

This activity can be used to develop the understanding of *quantitative aspects of numbers and counting.* Position and sequence is important in basic mathematics concepts. In this dance activity children can be helped to see the quantitative aspects of ordinal numbers, and the subtraction concept may also be introduced through this activity.

In the second example, five children stand on a line. The activity is called *Five Little Birds.* All of the children sing the verse to a melody made up by the teacher with the help of the children. The child whose number is repeated "flies" to a point a short distance away. This is continued until all of the "birds" have "flown" to the given point.

Five little birdies peeping through a door,
One went in and then there were four.
Four little birdies sitting in a tree,
One fell down and then there were three.
Three little birdies looking straight at you,
One went away and then there were two.
Two little birdies sitting in the sun,
One went home and then there was one.
One little birdie left all alone,
He flew away and then there were none.

If desired the following two verses can also be used.:

Five little chickadees pecking at my door.
One flew away, now there are four.
Four little chickadees very 'fraid of me,
One flew away, now there are three.
Three little chickadees didn't know what to do,
One flew away, now there are two.
One little chickadee hopping on the ground,
He flew away and now none are around.

In this verse they do not "fly," but move like bunnies:

Five little bunnies hopping on the floor,
One hops away and then there are four.
Four little bunnies sitting near a tree,
One hops away and then there are three.
Three little bunnies looking at you,
One hops away and then there are two.
One little bunny left all alone,
He hops away and then there are none.
All the little bunnies happy and gay,
All the little bunnies hop away.

As a child participate in this activity he dramatizes and acts out the concept of *one less than*. This method of introducing this concept to young children has been found to be much more effective than trying to verbalize it to them.

MATHEMATICS DANCE ACTIVITY STORIES

Another way in which children can derive mathematics experiences through dance activities is by use of the Mathematics Dance Activity Story. This procedure involves essentially the same kind of technique that was described in the previous chapter. A story involving the concept of number and oriented to the performance of a dance activity is written at the readability level for a specific group of children. The children may read the story themselves or the teacher may read it to them. Teachers who have experimented with this technique tend to feel that the best results are obtained when the story is read to the children. The reason for this is that with some children the internalization of the mathematical concept(s) in a story may be too difficult. It appears that certain children cannot handle the task of reading while at the same time developing an understanding of the mathematical aspect of the story.

Thus, the following instructions are submitted for use of the mathematics dance activity stories that appear in this chapter. In preparing to use a given story, the teacher should first read carefully all of the information connected with it. This information consists of (1) a story written at a specific reading level, (2) the mathematical skills, concepts, and learnings inherent in the story, and (3) suggested ways of developing the skills, concepts, and learnings with children.

Before having the children listen to the story, the teacher should attempt to determine the amount of teacher guidance that will be necessary. This may range from little or no teacher guidance to a considerable amount of teacher participation, depending of course upon the particular group of children. The teacher may wish to reproduce the story and have children read it after they participate in the activity (AMAV). It has been found in some cases that children can improve their comprehension skills as well as learn the mathematical concepts through this procedure.

Because of their own individual differences, I would emphasize that it is unnecessary for teachers to rely entirely on the above instructions. Some teachers have had greatest success in using the materials as an introduction to certain concepts. Others find the materials valuable in reinforcing certain concepts after they have been introduced. Still others have found it best to use this approach almost entirely, in particular when dealing with slow-learning children. It is hoped that teachers will draw upon their own resourcefulness, ingenuity, and imagination as they prepare to use the materials that follow:

MOVE LIKE ANIMALS

(Sung to the tune of "The Old Grey Mare.")
Let's all try to move like animals,
Move like animals,
Move like animals.
Let's all try to move like animals.
Like the animals do.

The following is narrated:
We try to move like animals. We move like a bear. We move like an elephant. We move like a frog. Try to move like these three animals. Take 5 steps like a bear. Take 4 steps like an elephant. Take 2 jumps like a frog. Now do it the other way. Take 2 jumps like a frog. Take 4 steps like an elephant. Take 5 steps like a bear. You did it the other way. You did the same number of steps and jumps. Do it in other ways. Move like other animals.

Mathematical Skills and Concepts
Commutative law
Addition
Rational counting
Quantitative concept of numbers

Reading Level
1.7 (7th month of first grade)

Teaching Suggestions
1. The children can count the animal movements as they make them. Also they can add these as they make them.
2. To show the quantitative concept of numbers it can be explained that when they take five steps like a bear they are doing five of something. Quantitative concepts of other numbers can also be explained in this manner after doing the activity.
3. To reinforce the understanding of commutative law the teacher can put 5 + 4 + 2 and 2 + 4 + 5 on flash cards before and/or after the activity.

TAKE AWAY, TAKE AWAY

Children stand in a ring. One child is "It." This child walks or skips around the ring. All children sing this song. Sing it like you would sing "Twinkle Twinkle Little Star."

Take away, take away, take away one.
Come with me and have some fun.
Take away, take away, take away two.
Come with me, oh yes please do.
Take away, take away, take away three.
All please come and skip with me.

Now sing and dance. This is what "It" does while all sing. "It" takes away one child by tapping him. He follows behind "It." Sing until "It" taps three children. At the end of the song all three try to get back to their places. "It" tries to get a place. Tell how many are left each time "It" takes away one child. Sing and dance again.

Mathematical Skills and Concepts   *Reading Level*
Subtraction   1.8
Groups or sets of 2 or 3

Teaching Suggestions
  1. Be sure the children know how many there are at the start.
  2. If the teacher wishes, the activity can be stopped each time after they sing to make it easier to tell how many are left.
  3. After two children have been taken·away it can be shown that they are now a group. This can also be shown after three are taken.

THE MULBERRY DANCE
  Do you know the song about the Mulberry Bush? Here are some new words to it.

Two plus (3 and 4) will make nine.
All will make nine, all will make nine.
Four plus (3 and 2) will make nine.
Either way you do it.

Sing the song. Think about the numbers. Think how they are placed. $2 + (3 + 4) = 9$, $4 + (3 + 2) = 9$. Think how they make nine. Now do this dance as you sing the song. Sing it three times. Children stand in two lines. The lines face each other. Sing the song once. Partners clap hands as they sing. Sing the song again. Take partner's hands and swing around. Sing the song again. Skip away with your partner. Sing the song three times. Do the whole dance again.

Mathematical Skills and Concepts	*Reading Level*
Associative law	1.9
Addition combinations	

Teaching Suggestions

1. *In developing the concept of the associative law flash cards or the chalkboard can be used for the combination: 2 + (3 + 4) = 9 and 4 + (3 + 2) = 9. The placement of the numbers can be used in this manner before and/or after the activity.*

2. *The above procedure can also be used for the addition combinations.*

COME AND DANCE WITH ME

Here is a song to sing as you dance. It is a little bit like "Farmer in the Dell." Here is the song:

Part 1. Oh, come and dance with me.
Oh, come and dance with me.
I take three to come with me.
Oh, come and dance with me.
Part 2. We all will stand in threes.
We all will stand in threes.
Oh, now we are together.
And we all stand in threes.
Part 3. We now go back you see.
We now go back you see.
Back to make our ring again.
And move around with glee.

The children stand in a ring. They hold hands. One child stands in the center. Sing the song and do what it says. Remember, the child in the center always takes three children. Sing Part 1 until all are taken. Sing Part 2 as all stand in the center. Sing Part 3 as all go back to the ring again.

Mathematical Skills and Concepts   *Reading Level*
Groups or sets of 3   1.9
Sequence of numbers

Teaching Suggestions

1. The idea of groups or sets of three can be seen as the children "stand in threes" during Part 2. In some cases it might be well to stop and point this out after Part 2 is sung.

2. The teacher can indicate sequence of numbers as they sing the parts of the song.

SING AND TAP

It takes seven children to do this dance. Six of the children hold hands to make a ring. Now sing this song. Sing it to the tune of "London Bridge is Falling Down."

> One plus two plus three make six.
> All make six, all make six.
> Three plus two plus one make six.
> Make six also.

The six children move around the ring as they sing. The other child moves around in the ring. The children stoop down when the song ends. The child in the ring tries to tap someone. He tries to tap a child before he gets down. Think of the way the numbers are as you sing. $1 + 2 + 3 = 6$, $3 + 2 + 1 = 6$. Think how they are changed but still make six. Ask another child to go in the ring. Dance again.

Mathematical Skills and Concepts   *Reading Level*
Commutative law   2.1
Addition

Teaching Suggestions

1. To reinforce the understanding of commutative law the teacher can put $1 + 2 + 3 = 6$ and $3 + 2 + 1 = 6$ on flash cards before and/or after the activity.

2. The above procedure can also be used for the addition combinations.

DANCE AROUND THE RING

Have three children stand together. Have three more children stand with them. Now have three more children join them. All hold hands and make a ring. Now you are ready to sing and dance. Sing this song to the tune of "Rock-A-Bye Baby."

If you take three and add on three more
You will have six you know I am sure.
Again you add three and now you will find
That with these three threes you now have nine.

Sing the song through three times. When you sing it the *first* time you move around the ring. When you sing it the *second* time you move to the center of the ring and back. When you sing it the *third* time you skip around the ring. Sing the song three times as you dance. Think of the numbers as you sing and dance.

Mathematical Skills and Concepts   *Reading Level*
Multiplication is a short way to   2.8
add
Groups or sets of 3
Ordinal numbers

Teaching Suggestions

1. The multiplication concept can be developed as the children see three groups of three, i.e., three threes make nine.

2. As three children are taken together it can be pointed out that they make a group of three.

3. Flash cards can be made with the ordinals First, Second, and Third on them. If it seems useful the teacher can hold up the flash cards as the song is sung the first, second and third time.

I highly recommend that teachers draw upon their own ingenuity and creativity to prepare dance activity stories. One reason for this is the paucity of published materials in this general area. In addition, teachers themselves can provide materials to meet the specific needs and interests of children in a given situation. Of course, there is one serious drawback to this: preparation of such materials is so time-consuming that it becomes more expedient to use professionally prepared materials, when they are available. It has been my experience, however, that those teachers who have the ability and have been willing to take the time have produced amazingly creative stories by using various dance settings and themes.

CHAPTER 11

IMPROVING CHILD LEARNING ABILITY THROUGH DANCE ACTIVITIES

In Chapter 4, in discussing the branches of dance, I made a comparison between compensatory dance and cognitive dance. It was indicated that although these two branches of dance are based essentially on the same concept, compensatory dance is concerned with education *of* the physical while cognitive dance is concerned with education *through* the physical. The previous two chapters involved the use of cognitive dance and this final chapter discusses the use of compensatory dance to improve the learning ability of children.

How does one go about improving a child's ability to learn using dance activities? First, something needs to be known about the abilities that need to be improved for desirable and worthwhile learning to take place. Generally, these abilities can be classified under the broad area of *perceptual-motor* abilities. To understand the meaning of perceptual-motor we first need to define the terms *perception* and *motor* separately, and then derive a meaning when these two terms are used together.

Perception is the process of obtaining information through the senses and organizing it. For present purposes the term *motor* is concerned with the impulse for motion, resulting in change of position through the various forms of body movement. When the two terms are combined (perceptual-motor), this refers to the organization of the information received through one or more of the senses, along with related voluntary motor responses.

The development of perceptual-motor abilities in children is referred to by some child development specialists as the process of providing "learning to learn" activities. This means improvement of such perceptual-motor qualities as *body awareness, laterality* and *directionality, auditory, visual, kinesthetic* and *tactile* perception skills. A deficiency in one or more of these can detract from a child's ability to learn.

It is the purpose here to help the reader determine whether such deficiencies exist, along with recommended dance experiences to help improve upon them. Even if no serious deficiency exists in any of these factors, the dance experiences suggested can still be used to sharpen and improve these skills, which are so important to learning.

IMPROVING BODY AWARENESS THROUGH DANCE ACTIVITIES

On this subject there are a number of terms that have been used to convey essentially the same meaning. Among others, these include body awareness, body schema, body image, body concept, body sense, and body experience. Regardless of which term is used, they all are likely to be concerned with the ability of the child to distinguish the particular features of the body parts. I prefer to use the term *body awareness.*

Most child development specialists tend to agree that a child's knowledge of the names and function of the various body parts is a very important factor in the improvement of learning ability. For example, body awareness gives a child a better understanding of the space his body takes and the relationship of its parts. Incidentally, these are critical factors in building foundations of mathematics competency.

It is doubtful that there are any absolutely foolproof methods of detecting problems of body awareness in children. The reason for this is that many things that are said to indicate such problems can also be symptoms of other deficiencies. Nevertheless, teachers should be on the alert to detect certain possible deficiencies.

In general, there are two ways in which deficiencies in body awareness might be detected. First, some deficiencies can be noticed by observing certain behaviors; second, there are some relatively simple diagnostic techniques that can be used to detect such deficiencies. The following generalized list contains examples of both of these possibilities and is presented to assist the teacher in this particular regard.

1. One technique often used to diagnose possible problems of body awareness is to have children make a drawing of themselves. The main reason for this is to see if certain parts of the body are *not* included in the drawing. Since the child's interest in drawing a man dates from his earliest attempts to represent things symbolically, it is possible, through typical drawings of young children, to trace certain characteristic stages of perceptual development. It has also been found that the procedure of drawing a picture of himself assists in helping to detect if there is a lack of body awareness.

2. Sometimes the child with a lack of body awareness may show tenseness in his movements. At the same time he may be unsure of his movements as he attempts to move the body segments (arm or leg).

3. If the child is instructed to move a body part such as placing one foot forward, he may direct this attention to the body part before making the movement; or, he may look at another child to observe the movement before he attempts to make the movement himself. (This could also be because of not understanding the instructions for the movement.)

4. When instructed to use one body part (arm) he may move the corresponding body part (other arm) when it is not necessary. For example, he may be asked to swing the left arm and may also start

to swing the right arm at the same time. (Items 2, 3 and 4 can be readily observed in certain dance activities.)

Dance Experiences Involving Body Awareness

Generally speaking, it might be said that when a child is given the opportunity to use his body freely as is the case with dance experiences, an increase in body awareness occurs. More specifically, there are certain activities that can be useful in helping children identify and understand the use of various body parts as well as the relationship of these parts. Over a period of time I have conducted a number of experiments to determine the effect of participating in certain dance experiences on body awareness. The following have proved to be very useful for this purpose.

CREATIVE DANCE

A very important activity for children with learning disabilities is creative dance, where the child responds by expressing himself in a way that the accompaniment makes him feel. When a child is able to use his body freely as in creative dance there is a strong likelihood that there will be increased body awareness. This also applies when creative dance gives the child self-direction in space, as well as self-control, in that he is not involved with a partner in a more formalized dance activity. It has been found that creative dance provides a situation for children with body awareness problems where they cannot fail. There are no rules to remember and no criteria for good or bad; the only things he is asked to do is create his own ideas. (The reader is referred to Chapter 7 on creative dance for examples to use in improving body awareness.)

STRUCTURED DANCES

Although great emphasis has been placed upon creative dance for the child with a body awareness problem, this should in no way minimize the value and importance of performing dances which are within the framework of an established pattern. For example, the identification and use of certain parts of the body, such as arms, hands, feet, and legs, are essential in some dances. Being called upon to use parts of the body may help establish one's awareness of body and body parts. The following examples are presented for this purpose.

LOOBY LOO

Verse

1. Here we dance Looby Loo, here we dance Looby Light.
2. Here we dance Looby Loo, all on a Saturday night.
3. I put my right hand in, I take my right hand out.
4. I give my right hand a shake, shake, shake, and turn myself about
(turn around in place)
I put my left hand in, etc.
I put my right foot in, etc.
I put my left foot in, etc.

Action. The children form a single circle with hands joined. On lines 1 and 2 of the verse the children walk three steps into the circle and three steps back, and repeat. As the rest of the lines are sung, the children do the actions indicated by the words. For example, with "I put my right hand in," they lean forward, extend the right hand and point it toward the center of the circle. At the end of each verse the children repeat the first verse again, taking three steps in and three steps out. The procedure can be continued with other parts of the body as desired, ending with "I put my whole self in," and so on. (Take a short jump in.)
Comment. In a discussion before participation in this activity the teacher can be sure the children are aware of the body part and when to activate it. In addition, the activity can serve well as an evaluative device for the teacher to see how well the children are aware of the various body parts.

BIG BEE

Verse

1. Up on toes, back on heels
2. Hands on head, see how it feels.
3. Bend at the waist, touch your knees.
4. Skip around if you please.
5. Keep on skipping around the ring.
6. Look out for the Big Bee sting.

Action. All the children except one who is *Big Bee* form a circle. Big Bee stands inside the circle and close to the children in the circle. The children execute the action indicated in the verse as they sing it. On line 4 they skip around the circle clockwise. Big Bee walks around in the circle counterclockwise. At the end of the last word of the verse all of the children in the circle stoop down. Big Bee tries to tag (sting) one of the children in the circle before that child assumes the stooping position. A new Big Bee is selected and the activity continues.

Comment. After explaining and discussing the actions that the children are to execute, the extent to which they are able to identify the various body parts concerned can be observed. In evaluating the activity with the children the teacher can ask where a child was *stung*, "On the arm?" "On the leg?" etc.

IMPROVING LATERALITY AND DIRECTIONALITY THROUGH DANCE ACTIVITIES

Laterality and directionality are inherent aspects of body awareness. Thus, progress towards greater differentiation within body awareness and function begins with the learned ability to discriminate between the left and right sides of the body. It is well known that the bilaterality symmetrical placement of the limbs, the sense receptors, and the nerve pathways play a significant part in this process. As the child develops a preference for handedness or footedness, it becomes easier for him to distinguish between the two sides of the body. As laterality develops the child begins to apply his learned concepts of *right* and *left* in the location of near objects. The progression here is not automatic, since the learning of *directionality* is preceded by the complex process of learning to integrate the visual information of external objects with the established kinesthetic awareness on which the child has built his concept of *laterality*. Thus, development of laterality precedes development of directionality, since the child learns to translate the right–left discrimination within himself into right–left discrimination among objects outside himself.[1]

Laterality is an internal awareness of the left and right sides of the body in relation to the child himself. It is concerned with the child's knowledge of how each side of the body is used separately or together. Directionality is the projection into space of laterality; that is, the awareness of left and right, up and down, over and under, etc., in the world around the child. Stated in another way, directionality in space is the ability to project outside the body the laterality that the child has developed within himself.

The qualities of laterality and directionality make up the broader classification of *directional awareness*. The development of this quality is most important in that it is an essential element for reading and writing. These two basic "R"'s require that the hand and/or eyes be moved from left to right in a coordinated manner. Also, interpretation of left and right directions is an important requirement for the child in dealing with the environment. It is interesting to note that some children who have *not* developed laterality quite often will write numbers sequentially from left to right. However, when doing addition and subtraction they may want to start from the left instead of the right. Dance activities designed to differentiate right and left sides of the body can be an important part of remedial arithmetic.

Since laterality and directionality are important aspects of body awareness, some of the methods of detecting deficiencies in body awareness mentioned earlier also apply here. In addition, it may be noted that the child is inclined to use just the dominant side of his

[1] P. R. Morris, and H. T. A. Whiting, *Motor Impairment and Compensatory Education,* (Philadelphia, Lea & Febiger, 1971), p. 224.

body. Also, confusion may result if the child is given directions for body movements that call for a specific direction in which he is to move. (The reader is asked to refer back to the discussion on directionality of sound in Chapter 3.)

Some specialists have indicated that they have had success with a specific test of laterality. This test is given on a 4-inch wide walking board that is 2 feet in length. The child tries to walk forward, backward, and sideways, right to left and left to right, while attempting to maintain his balance. It is likely that a child with laterality problems will experience difficulty moving in one of the sideways directions, ordinarily from left to right.

Dance Experiences Involving Laterality and Directionality

Dancing can involve left and right directionality and at times may involve constant changing of directions. A case in point is the "Children's Polka" described in Chapter 8. This dance provides many opportunities for the children to change direction while at the same time performing a coordinated movement with the hands, such as clapping their own hands as well as their partners' hands. As the children learn the activity the teacher can stress the terms *right* and *left* since they are used in directions for sliding. In all structured dance activities such as this the teacher might take note of those children who are depending upon others for directions. This could indicate that these children are having more pronounced problems of laterality and/or directionality. Thus, structured dance activities can serve as a diagnostic technique. Following are some representative examples of dance activities that can be used to improve upon laterality and/or directionality. (The first two are in story form.)

THE TOY SOLDIER

I am a toy soldier.
I can march.
This is how I march
I stand tall.
I swing my arms.

I keep my knees straight.
I raise my feet high.
I keep time with my feet.
I say:
  "Left, right.
  Left, right.
  Left, right.
  Left, right."
I march and march.
Could you march like a toy soldier?

WE MAKE UP A DANCE

One day Miss Jones asked the children
  in her class if they would like to
  make up a dance.
The children were very happy because
  they liked to dance.
They thought they could start the dance
  by holding hands and making a circle.
After they made the circle, they all sang.
Let us slide to the right.
Let us slide, slide, slide.
Let us slide to the left.
Let us slide, slide, slide.
Now let us turn to the right all the way around.
Now let us turn to the left and all sit down.
Could you get some other children
to help work out this dance?

HICKORY DICKORY DOCK

Verse

1. Hickory Dickory Dock.
2. The mouse ran up the clock.

3. The clock struck one!
4. Watch the mouse run!
5. Hickory Dickory Dock.

Action. The children form a double circle with partners facing. On line 1 the hands are in front of the body to form pendulums and the arms are swung left and right. On line 2 partners change places with six short running steps. On line 3 they clap hands over head. On line 4 they go back to their original place with six short running steps. On line 5 they swing the arms as in line 1.

Comment. The teacher should observe the smoothness of the arm movements as the children swing the arms, and whether or not the children are following the directions. After line 2 the positions of the children should be noted to make sure that they have made the correct movement. Certain words, such as *up,* can be emphasized as directional terms.

LONDON BRIDGE
(Also see *Sing and Tap* in Chapter 10)

Verse

1. London Bridge is falling down, falling down, falling down.
2. London Bridge is falling down, my fair lady.

Action. Two children stand facing each other, hands clasped and arms extended overhead to form an arch or bridge. The other children form a line holding hands. They walk around under the bridge. On the words "my fair lady," the two who have formed the bridge (bridge tenders) let their arms drop, catching the child who happens to be passing under at the time. The bridge tenders then ask him to choose something that each of the tenders represent, such as gold or silver. The child caught stands behind the bridge tender who represents gold or silver as the case may be. The activity proceeds until all have been caught and the side with the most children wins. There should not be too many children in the line in order to avoid a long wait for the children caught.

Comment. This activity gives two children (bridge tenders) an opportunity to focus on the child (object) when they drop their arms to catch the child passing under at the time. The word *down* in the verse is emphasized. When the teacher evaluates the activity with the children the directions used can be brought out.

HOW D'YE DO, MY PARTNER

Verse.

1. How d'ye do, my partner.
2. How are you today?
3. Shall we dance in a circle?
4. I will show you the way.
5. Tra la la la la la, etc. (chorus)

Action. The following actions are performed with the singing accompaniment. A double circle is formed, girls on the outside and boys on the inside. Partners face each other and bow. Partners join inside hands and skip counterclockwise around the circle during the chorus. On the last two measures of the chorus the boys move ahead one person and continue to dance with a new partner.

Comment. Each child gets an opportunity to skip with a partner in a given direction. The teacher should observe closely for those boys who do not move forward to the new partner at the proper time. They must coordinate the timing of the verse with the appropriate time to move ahead one person.

IMPROVING THE FORMS OF PERCEPTION THROUGH DANCE ACTIVITIES

At the beginning of this chapter I defined perception as the process of obtaining information through the senses and organizing it. However, this term is often defined differently by different sources. For example, one source describes perception as an individual's awareness of and reaction to stimuli.[2] A second source refers to it as the process by which the individual maintains contact with his environment.[3] And still another source describes it as the mental interpretation of the messages received through the senses.[4]

According to Piaget[5] perception is developmental; that is, it changes with age and experience, and development is continuous and quantitative. Development of perception occurs in three major periods: (1) sensorimotor intelligence, which occurs during the period between birth to about two years, involves learning to coordinate various perceptions and movements; (2) the ages from two to about eleven or twelve involve preparation for and organization of concrete operations, as well as the acquisition of language (it is during this period that the child learns to deal logically with his surroundings); and (3) formal operations, which occur after the age of eleven or twelve, and has to do with the development of abstract and formal systems.

Some of the senses most involved in learning are *auditory* perception, *visual* perception, *kinesthetic* perception, and *tactile* perception all of which play an important role in learning. The following discussions are concerned with how these forms of perceptions relate to dance experiences.

Auditory Perception

It was estimated many years ago that about 75 percent of the waking hours is spent in verbal communication—45 percent in listening, 30 percent in speaking, 16 percent in reading, and the remaining 9 percent in writing.[6] If this estimate can be used as a valid criterion, the importance of development of listening skills cannot be denied. If

[2] Robert E. Silverman, *Psychology*, 2nd ed., (New York, Appleton-Century-Crofts, 1974), p. 151.
[3] R. H. Day, *Perception*, (Dubuque: William C. Brown Publishers, 1966), p. 1.
[4] Donald C. Cushenbery and Kenneth J. Gilbreath, *Effective Reading Instruction for Slow Learners*, (Springfield, Ill.: Charles C. Thomas, 1972), p. 98.
[5] Jean Piaget, *Les Méchanismes Perceptifs*, (Paris, Presses Universitares de France, 1961).
[6] George D. Spache, *Toward Better Reading*, (Champaign, Ill.: Garrard Publishing Company, 1963), p. 181.

children are going to learn to listen effectively, care should be taken to improve their auditory perception—the mental interpretation of what a person hears. (Before reading further it might be well to review the material in Chapter 3 on auditory input.)

There are a variety of opportunities for children to improve their auditory perception through dance activities. Perhaps the most natural way involves the various forms of accompaniment. That is, the child listens to accompaniment which in most dance activities helps guide him in the dance experience. Also, in those dance forms such as square dance the child needs to listen to the calls in executing the dance.

In activities such as movement songs where accompaniment is furnished through song, it is the auditory clues that guide movement. Thus, an opportunity is provided for auditory discrimination.

The child first learns to act on the basis of verbal instructions by others. In this regard it has long been known that later he learns to guide and direct his own behavior on the basis of his own language activities—he literally talks to himself, giving himself instructions. Speech as a form of communication between children and adults thus later becomes a means of organizing the child's own behavior. The function which was previously divided between two people, child and adult, later becomes an internal function of human behavior. Hence the importance of dance activities where children furnish their own accompaniment through song.

Visual Perception

Visual perception can be described as the mental interpretation of what a person sees. Some of the aspects of visual perception that have been identified include eye–motor coordination, figure–ground perception, form constancy, position in space, and spatial relationships. It has been suggested that children who show deficiency in these various areas may have difficulty with school performance. (The reader might wish to review the material in Chapter 3 on visual input.)

Many of the movement songs and other structured dance forms can provide opportunities for training in figure–ground relationships and improvement in form perception. In addition to the development of forms in certain dance patterns, the different formations for dances such as line, circle, and square are useful experiences for children.

Numerous dances provide for eye–hand and eye–foot coordination and, as such, are valuable experiences in developing those forms of visual perception. A specific example is the dance *Children's Polka* described in Chapter 8.

Kinesthetic Perception

Kinesthetic perception can be described as the mental interpretation of the sensation of movement. In summarizing a number of definitions of the term *kinesthesis*, Joseph Oxendine[7] suggests that the following four factors seem to be constant, thus emphasizing the likeness of the various definitions: (1) position of body segments, (2) precision of movement, (3) balance, and (4) space orientation.

In attempting to diagnose deficiencies in kinesthetic sensitivity, teachers should resort to the observation of certain behaviors and mannerisms of children. They should be on the alert to observe those children who have difficulty with motor coordination; that is, difficulty using the muscles in such a manner that they work together effectively. Such lack of coordination may be seen with children who have difficulty in performing the locomotor movements that involve an uneven rhythm (skipping, galloping, and sliding) described in Chapter 6.

Since balance is an important aspect of kinesthesis, simple tests for balance can be administered to determine if there is a lack of proficiency. One such test would be to have the child stand on either foot. Normally, a child should be able to maintain such a position for a period of about ten seconds.

The importance of kinesthetic perception in dance should be obvious, since all dance activities involve movement of some sort. In this regard those receptors responsible for informing the body of its conscious change in position as well as the relationship of its parts

---

[7] Joseph Oxendine, *Psychology of Motor Learning*, (New York: Appleton-Century-Crofts, 1968), p. 291.

in space have been demonstrated to be necessary in the smooth movements of skilled acts. In view of this, practically all forms of dance activities are useful in the improvement of kinesthetic sensitivity.

There are certain types of dance activities that can make the child aware of the movements of certain muscle groups. Two such examples are *We Dance* and *Around the Ring,* both described in Chapter 9. In these activities the teacher can evaluate the experience with the children by questioning them about what they did. Also the activities can be repeated to see if the children show improvement in understanding the muscle groups involved in the performance of the dances.

Tactile Perception

The tactile sense is so closely related to the kinesthetic sense that the two are often confused. One of the main reasons for this is that the ability to detect changes in touch (tactile) involves many of the same receptors concerned with informing the body of changes in its position. The essential difference between the tactile sense and the kinesthetic sense may be seen in the definitions of these two forms of perception. Kinesthetic perception involves the mental correlation and interpretation of movement within the sensory realms of proprioception (tactile sensation of one's own muscles), balance, and space orientation; whereas tactile perception is concerned with the mental interpretation of what a person experiences through the sense of touch alone, whether or not there is any movement.

A number of elementary diagnostic techniques for tactile sensitivity can be played in a game-type situation so that the child is unaware of being tested. The following list suggests some representative examples.

1. Have the child explore the surface and texture of objects in the classroom. Determine if he can differentiate among these objects.
2. Evaluate the child's past experience by having him give the names of two or three hard objects, two or three rough objects, and so on.
3. Some classroom teachers have had successful experience with the

learning box idea; that is, in this case a *touching box* can be developed with the use of an ordinary shoebox in which are placed different shaped objects and different textured objects. The child reaches into the box without looking and feels the various objects to see if he can identify them.

Practically all dance activities are useful in the improvement of tactile sensitivity, particularly movement songs and other structured dance forms. In these kinds of activities the entire group, or partners, move in various patterns with hands joined. In addition, various forms of body contact are involved in swinging a partner, clapping hands with a partner, and the like. Two examples of these follow.

CHARLIE OVER THE WATER

Verse

1. Charlie over the water.
2. Charlie over the sea.
3. Charlie caught a blackbird.
4. Can't catch me.

Action. One child is selected to be Charlie. The rest of the children form a circle and join hands. Charlie stands about two or three feet inside the circle. As the verse is sung, the children comprising the circle move around counterclockwise while Charlie moves inside the circle clockwise. On the last word of the verse, all of the children stoop down. Charlie tries to tag the nearest child before he or she gets down. The activity continues with another child selected as Charlie.

RABBIT IN THE HOLLOW

Verse

1. Rabbit in the hollow sits and sleeps.

2. Hunter in the forest nearer creeps.
3. Little rabbit, have a care.
4. Deep within your hollow there.
5. Quickly to the forest,
6. You must run, run, run.

Action. The children form a circle with hands joined. One child, taking the part of the rabbit, crouches inside the circle while another child, taking the part of the hunter, stands outside the circle. A space nearby is designated as the rabbit's home, to which he may run and in which he is safe. On lines 1 and 2 the children in the circle move clockwise. On lines 3 and 4 the children in the circle stand still and the rabbit tries to get away from the hunter by breaking through the circle and attempting to reach home without being tagged. If the rabbit is tagged, he chooses another child to be the rabbit. The hunter chooses another hunter.

Throughout this book I have attempted to demonstrate the importance that dance experiences can have in the lives of children. To this end, many aspects of dance for children have been taken into account and discussed in some detail. However, it will remain the responsibility of creative teachers to expand upon these ideas and concepts and to draw upon their own ingenuity to provide for the most desirable and worthwhile dance learning experiences for children.

APPENDIX

Record Sources
1. Bowmar Records, Department J-569, 622 Rodier Driver, Glendale, CA 91201.
2. Canadian F. D. S., Educational Recordings, 605 King Street W., Toronto, 2B, Canada.
3. Children's Music Center, Inc., 5373 West Pico Boulevard, Los Angeles, CA 90019.
4. Dance Record Center, 1161 Broad Street, Newark, NJ 07114.
5. David McKay, Inc., 750 Third Avenue, New York, NY 10017.
6. Electronic Records for Children, Box 185, Kingsbridge Station, Bronx, NY 10463.
7. Educational Activities, Inc., Box 392, Freeport, NY 11520.
8. Educational Recordings of America, Inc., Box 231, Monroe, CT 06468.
9. Educational Record Sales, 157 Chambers Street, New York, NY 10007.
10. Folkraft Records, 1159 Broad Street, Newark, NJ 07114.
11. Freda Miller Records for Dance, Department J, Box 383, Northport, Long Island, NY 11768.
12. Hoctor Educational Records, Inc., Waldwick, NJ 07463.
13. Instructor Publications, Inc., Dansville, NY 14437.
14. Kimbo Educational, Box 477, 10 North Third Avenue, Long Branch, NJ 07740.
15. Loshin's, 215 East Eighth Street, Cincinnati, OH 45202.
16. Master Record Service, 708 East Garfield, Phoenix, AZ 85000.
17. McDonald & Evans, Ltd., 8 John Street, London WC1, UK.
18. Merrback Records Service, Box 7308, Houston, TX 77000.

19. RCA Victor, Education Department J, 155 East 24th Street, New York, NY 10010.
20. Record Center, 2581 Piedmont Road N.E., Atlanta, GA 30324.
21. Rhythms Production Records, Department J, Box 34485 Los Angeles, CA 90034.
22. Rhythm Record Company, 9203 Nichols Road, Oklahoma City, OK 73120.
23. Russell Records, Box 3318, Ventura, CA 91403.
24. S & R Records, 1609 Broadway, New York, NY 10017.
25. Square Dance Square, Box 689, Santa Barbara, CA 93100.
26. Standard Records & Hi Fi Company, 1028 N.E. 65th, Seattle, WA 98115.
27. Windsor Records, 5530 N. Rosemead Boulevard, Temple City, CA 91780.
28. Young People's Records, % Living Language, 100 Sixth Avenue, New York, NY 10013.

BIBLIOGRAPHY

Abeles, Jeanette and McDoll, Sharon, eds. *Creative Dance Starters: Quick and Easy Lessons for the Elementary Classroom.* East Lansing, Michigan Dance Association, 1979.

American Alliance for Health, Physical Education, Recreation and Dance. *Children's Dance.* 2nd ed., Reston Va., 1981.

American Alliance for Health, Physical Education, Recreation and Dance. *Dance as Learning.* Reston, Va., 1980.

American Alliance for Health, Physical Education and Recreation. *Dance as Education.* Washington, D.C., 1977.

Bain, Linda L. "A Dancing Spirit." *Journal of Physical Education, Recreation and Dance,* September, 1984.

Barlin, Anne and Barlin, Paul. *Dance-a-Folk Song.* Los Angeles, Bowmar, 1974.

Bauer, Lois M. *Dance and Play Activities for the Elementary Grades.* New York, Chartwell House, 1971.

Boorman, Joyce. *Dance and Language Experiences with Children.* Hamilton, Ont., Longman Canada, 1973.

Boorman, Joyce. *Creative Dance in Grades Four to Six.* Hamilton, Ont., Longman Canada, 1971.

Boorman, Joyce. *Creative Dance in the First Three Grades.* New York, David McKay, 1969.

Brennan, Mary Alice. "Relationship Between Creativity Ability in Dance and Selected Creative Attributes." *Perceptual and Motor Skills,* August, 1982.

Brown, C. Andrea. "Elementary School Dance—Teaching Rhythms and Education Forms." *Journal of Physical Education, Recreation and Dance,* February, 1986.

Carter, Curtis L. "The State of Dance in Education: Past and Present." *Theory into Practice,* Fall, 1984.

Carr, D. "Dance Education, Skill, and Behavioral Objectives." *Journal of Aesthetic Education*, Winter, 1984.

Carroll, Jean and Lofthouse, Peter. *Creative Dance for Boys*. New York International Publications Service, 1969.

Carver, V. M. "Aesthetic Concepts: A Paradigm for Dance." *Quest*, 37, No. 2, 1985.

Cunningham, J. "Dancin'!" *Instructor*, February, 1983.

Dimondstein, Geraldine. *Children Dance in the Classroom*. New York, Macmillan Publishing Co., 1971.

Docherty, David. *Education Through Dance Experience*. Bellington, Wash., Educational Designs and Consultants, 1975.

Doll, Edna and Nelson, Mary Jarmon. *Rhythms Today*. Morristown, N.J., Silver Burdett Company, 1965.

Farley, Pamela. *A Teacher's Guide to Creative Dance*. Sydney, Reed, 1969.

Fleming, Gladys Andrews. *Creative Rhythmic Movement*. Englewood Cliffs, N.J., Prentice-Hall, 1976.

Foster, John. *The Influence of Rudolph Laban*. London, Henry Kimpton, 1977.

Gelineau, R. Phyllis. *Songs in Action*. New York, McGraw-Hill, 1974.

Gilbert, Cecile. *International Folk Dance at a Glance*. 2nd ed., Minneapolis, 1974.

Goodridge, Janet. *Creative Dance and Improvised Movement for Children*. Boston, Plays, Inc., 1971.

Gray, Judith A. "A Conceptual Framework for the Study of Dance Teaching." *Quest*, 36, No. 2, 1984.

Gray, Judith A. "The Science of Teaching the Art of Dance: A Description of a Computer-Aided System for Recording and Analyzing Dance Instructional Behaviors." *Journal of Education for Teaching*, October, 1983.

Hankin, T. "Laban Movement Analysis in Dance Education." *Journal of Physical Education, Recreation and Dance*, November/December, 1984.

Harris, Jane, Pittman, Anne, and Waller, Marlys. *Dance a While*. Minneapolis, Burgess, 1978.

Heaton, Alma. *Fun Dance Rhythms*. Provo, Utah, Brigham Young University Press, 1976.

Hill, Rose. "The Importance of Dance Experiences and Concepts in the Aesthetic Development of Children. *Proceedings of the Canadian Association for Health, Physical Education and Recreation*, 1978.

Humphrey, James H. "Teaching Reading Through Creative Movement." *Academic Therapy*, Spring 1974.

Humphrey, James H. *Learning to Listen and Read Through Movement*. Long Branch, N.J., Kimbo Educational, 1974.

Humphrey, James H. *Teaching Children Mathematics Through Games, Rhythms and Stunts*. Long Branch, N.J., 1969.

Hsu, G. O. B. "Movement and Dance Are Child's Play." *Music Education*, May, 1981.

Hanna, Judith Lynne. "Mentality and Matter of Dance." *Art Education*, March, 1983.

Jensen, Mary Bee, and Jensen, Clayne R. *Square Dancing*. Provo, Utah, Brigham Young University Press, 1973.

Joyce, Mary. *Dance Techniques for Children*. Palo Alto, Cal., Mayfield Publishing Co., 1984.

Joyce, Mary. *First Steps in Teaching Creative Dance to Children*. 2nd ed., Palo Alto, Cal., Mayfield Publishing Co., 1980.

Kaplan, D. "Dancing in the Aisles." *Instructor*, October, 1980.

Laban, Rudolph. *Modern Educational Dance*. 3rd ed., London, McDonald & Evans, 1975.

Leslie, Laurel. "Toward Efficient Alignment: Dance Teachers Can Help." *Journal of Physical Education, Recreation and Dance*, April, 1986.

Leventhal, M. B. "Dance Therapy as a Treatment of Choice for the Emotionally Disturbed and Learning Disabled Child." *Journal of Physical Education Recreation and Dance*, September, 1980.

Lewis, Naima. "Dance: An Essential Educational Tool for the Future." *Teacher Education Quarterly*, Spring, 1983.

Lidster, Miriam and Tamburini, Dorothy. *Folk Dance Progressions*. Belmont, Cal., Wadsworth Publishing Co., 1965.

Logan, M. "Dance in the Schools: A Person Account." *Theory into Practice*. Autumn, 1984.

McFee, Graham. "Why Teach Dance to Children and Why Let Them See It." *Proceedings of the Canadian Association for Health, Physical Education, and Recreation*, 1978.

Magruder, E. "Imagery and Improvisation in Dance in the Schools." *Journal of Physical Education, Recreation and Dance*, March, 1981.

Maynard, Olga. *Children and Dance and Music*. New York, Scribner, 1968.

Mettler, Barbara. *Children's Creative Dance Book*. Tucson, Mettler Studios, 1970.

Mettler, Barbara. *Materials of Dance as a Creative Art*. Tucson, Mettler Studios, 1970.

Mettler, Barbara. *The Nature of Dance as a Creative Art Activity*, Tucson, Mettler Studios, 1980.

Murray, Ruth Lovell, *Dance in Elementary Education*. 3rd ed., New York, Harper & Row, 1975.

Nadel, M. H. "Dance and the New Magnet Schools." *Contemporary Education*, Fall, 1985.

Nelson, Esther L. *Dancing Games for Children of All Ages*. New York, Sterling Publishing Company, 1974.

Nelson, Esther L. *Holiday Singing & Dancing Games*. New York, Sterling Publishing Company, 1980.

Pruett, D. M. "Interactions: Elementary Schools with a University Dance

Company." *Journal of Physical Education, Recreation and Dance*, November/December, 1982.

Ramsay, J. M. "Folk Dancing is for Everyone." *Journal of Physical Education, Recreation and Dance*, September, 1984.

Redfern, Betty. "The Child as Creator, Performer, Spectator." *Proceedings of the Canadian Association for Health, Physical Education and Recreation*, 1978.

Russell, Joan. *Creative Movement and Dance for Children*. Boston, Plays, Inc., 1975.

Russell, Joan. *Creative Dance in the Primary School*. New York, Praeger Publishers, 1968.

Santa, D. M. "Dancing: An Important Step Toward Self Esteem." *Vocational Education*, June, 1980.

Sheehy, Erma. *Children Discover Music and Dance*. New York, Teacher's College Press, 1968.

Shreeves, Rosamund. Movement and Educational Dance for Children. Boston, Plays, Inc., 1979.

Stillwell, J. E. "How Do You Dance Brown?" *Art Teacher*, Fall, 1980.

Taylor, Carla. *Rhythm: A Guide for Creative Movement*. Mountain View, Cal., Peek Publications, 1973.

Trammell, P. "Poetry and Dance for Children." *Journal of Physical Education, Recreation and Dance*, March, 1983.

Wiener, Jack and Lidstone, John. *Creative Movement for Children: A Dance Program for the Classroom*. New York, Van Nostrand Reinhold, 1969.

Wilson, Robert M., Humphrey, James H., and Sullivan, Dorothy D. *Teaching Reading Through Creative Movement*. Long Branch, N.J., 1970.

Winters, Shirley. *Creative Rhythmic Movement for Children of Elementary School Age*. Dubuque, Ia., William C. Brown, Publishers, 1975.

Index